CONTROL GAMES

CONTROL GAMES

Avoiding Intimacy on the Singles Scene

Gerald Alper, M.S.

JASON ARONSON INC.
Northvale, New Jersey
London

This book was set in 12 pt. Bodoni Antiqua by Alpha Graphics of Pittsfield, New Hampshire and printed and bound by Book-mart Press of North Bergen, New Jersey.

Library of Congress Cataloging-in-Publication Data

Alper, Gerald.
 Control games : avoiding intimacy on the singles scene / Gerald Alper.
  p. cm.
 Includes bibliographical references and index.
 ISBN 1-56821-729-3 (alk. paper)
  1. Intimacy (Psychology) 2. Control (Psychology) 3. Manipulative behavior. 4. Single people—Psychology. I. Title.
 BF575.I5A445   1996
 158'.2—dc20   95-49764

Manufactured in the United States of America. Jason Aronson Inc. offers books and cassettes. For information and catalog write to Jason Aronson Inc., 230 Livingston Street, Northvale, New Jersey 07647.

To
Anita, Tom, and Steve

CONTENTS

3. RULES OF THE GAME 111

4. THERAPY 181

PREFACE

In 1953, in *The Interpersonal Theory of Psychiatry*, Harry Stack Sullivan outlined many of the ways an individual endeavors to anxiously control the level of self-esteem that he or she will eventually attain. Approximately ten years later, Eric Berne (1964), in *Games People Play*, emphasized the ways that people have to avoid intimacy by compulsively compartmentalizing their social interactions into game-like behaviors. Today, thirty years later, it is still fashionable to talk about the avoidance of intimacy and the alarming need for game-free behavior. And today, as before, the need for intimacy is quickly forgotten and the defensive, avoidant behavior as such—the games, in Eric Berne's system of transactional analysis and, in present-day jargon, the various pathological outcomes of the ubiquitous dysfunctional family—begins to take on a life of its own. Soon, what the defenses are for is not remembered, which makes it increasingly difficult to comprehend the real consequences and underlying significance of the symptoms. In their stead is a growing fascination with what could justifiably be designated the illness of our time—traumatized survivors of an abused childhood: adult children of alcoholics, of sexual molesters, of batterers, of narcissists, and so on. From that perspective, intimacy is acknowledged primarily by its absence, and, by subscribing to the belief that it can only developmentally arrive when the pathology is excised, it relegates it to a conveniently abstract future.

By contrast, the emphasis in this book is on what I consider to be the far greater psychical disaster (of which the particular attention-getting symptom is, after all, only a symptom)—the establishment of a non-intimate relationship. To highlight this, I always try to look at the behavior in question against the backdrop of, and in dynamic relation to, the intimacy that is being avoided, and I therefore put the main focus on *how* the specific control game functions to keep authentic interrelating at bay. By showing the individual dynamics of non-intimate control games in juxtaposition with the intimacy that is being denied, a much clearer picture is given than if one simply depicts a common dysfunctional behavior (e. g., addictive substance abuse) and then proceeds to chronicle the assorted physiological, social, economic, and mental features that typically are associated with it.

In ordinary language, when the term *control* is applied to psychology and characterology, it means one of two things: a controlling personality who feels anxious if his own agenda does not carry the day, or, by contrast, a person who seemingly is in command of himself and his situation in a way that is neither rigid nor unduly defensive. Historically, psychoanalytic ego psychology has conceptualized the latter as the reflection of a progressive integration and hierarchical adaptation of the psyche, which is considered to be healthy. (For example, Adam Phillips (1993), writing from the British object relations viewpoint in a recent brilliant essay, "On Composure," has presented a compelling developmental story of the vicissitudes of the individual's attempt to self-regulate the ego so as to keep it quiescent and in a holding state.) As for the controlling personality, much has been written under the category of the obsessive-compulsive disorder.

Although by no means do I wish to minimize the importance of the developmental or intrapsychic, the main emphasis throughout the book will be on the actual transactions that occur in the interpersonal realm. A primary reason is my belief that—in spite of the incessant commentary on dysfunctional, exploitative, and abusive relationships—there is at present an overwhelming neglect of the extent to which attempts to orchestrate the interaction between self and other have come to stand proxy for genuine relating. Such neglect may be seen in part as denial of the void that has been created by the profound and almost ubiquitous impairment of the ability to be intimate—a denial that has been abetted by the bewildering variety of interpersonal maneuvers or control games that continue to proliferate.

Elsewhere I have made explicit the disturbing connection that exists between an absence of intimacy and a need to control, but here it is enough to dwell on the details. Hence the phenomenological approach, with which I hope to recreate the flavor of what has essentially been passed over in the mental health field's rush to build fashionable theories purporting to explain whatever has been nominated as the latest and most heart-rending casualty of so-called dysfunctional relating: children of alcoholics, children of narcissists, children of abusive parents, and so forth. The focus usually is on either the shocking trauma or on the astonishingly dramatic recovery, but rarely on the underlying patterns of control that have become an unobtrusive, although permanent, feature in the mosaic of contemporary interrelating.

In an essay I once wrote, "The Theory of Games and Psychoanalysis" (Alper 1993), I outlined the position that I take here vis-à-vis contemporary game theory, to be located somewhere between the discrete behavioral series of moves seen in such classic games as "Prisoner's Dilemma" and the more psychodynamically oriented transactions portrayed memorably by Eric Berne in *Games People Play* (1964). This is because the psychodynamic patterns that emerge in the course of a psychoanalytic psychotherapy show neither the sequential behaviors of traditional game theorists nor the elegant convolutions of R. D. Laing's *Knots* (1970) or Berne's *Games People Play*.

They are instead, as I see them, rough-hewn psychodynamic strategies unconsciously enacted primarily to spare the person the imagined angst that would be stirred up by anything remotely approximating, at that particular dynamic moment in time, an authentic encounter. The control games that follow can be characterological but do not have to be; all people, even those rare individuals who are capable of ongoing intimacy, are forced at moments of frailty or interpersonal indecisiveness to play control games, and certainly the culture at large pervasively sponsors the enactment of opportunistic interpersonal strategies.

At the heart of this book is the assumption that there is a profound need in human beings for intimacy—one that is being massively frustrated in contemporary society. Such a need differs widely among individuals, is subject to familial, developmental vicissitudes, but is always there. A further assumption therefore—a consequence of the pathological inhibition against being intimate that is pervasive in our culture—is that with few exceptions, regardless of the level of interpersonal maturation attained by the individual, there will be a (healthy) need for more intimacy. In opposition to the current trend in psychiatric literature, in which non-intimate behavior is described as pathological or dysfunctional and intimacy is represented mainly in terms of its absence (as deprivation or arrest), the focus here is on what might be called *intimacy-hunger as an active agent.* The fact that this driving need to achieve some level of meaningful intimacy is widely and systematically frustrated in present-day society only serves to intensify the hunger. This does not mean that there are no people who do not, for developmental reasons, possess low intimacy needs. It does mean, if it is true (as I believe) that almost everyone suffers to some degree because of the profound barriers against being intimate that exist in our culture, then that fact must exert a dynamic impact on nearly all aspects of behavior.

Thirty years ago Eric Berne saw non-intimate, game-like behavior wherever he looked, but he had little trouble maintaining his sense of humor. Although he insisted that games are serious, he readily acknowledged that their retrospective analysis often evoked amusement in the actual participants. In the past thirty years, this tendency has only increased, leading to the irony that the presumably therapeutic analysis of the games people play, by being so gratifying and entertaining, begins more and more to serve the very end—avoidance of intimacy—for which the original games were unconsciously created.

As behavior becomes increasingly dysfunctional and society becomes increasingly narcissistic, patients become sicker and so do their games. In retrospect, Berne's games of thirty years ago—while still played today (e. g., "Yes, but")—seem by comparison refreshingly free of trauma. From an historical perspective, therefore, *Games People Play* can be looked upon as a child of its time—the psychotherapy equivalent of Camelot—the message being that if we just stop hurting one another, if we stop playing games, wake up and not only smell the roses but begin to appreciate and love one another, then a truly new, humanistic age could take shape.

Over thirty years later it is clear that it didn't happen that way. Today, perhaps more than ever before, people are struggling to control one another. If this is so it is better to know it, and in order to show it—from the vantage point and through the prism of psychoanalytic psychotherapy—I have written this book.

A final note: percipient readers of my previous books—*The Singles Scene: A Psychoanalytic Study of the Breakdown of Intimacy* and *The Puppeteers: Studies of Obsessive Control*—will realize that the present work is, in a sense, an amalgam of these two. It is also, however, an attempt to push further. Accordingly, the first chapter is an updated version of *Games People Play* for the '90s from a psychoanalytic point of view. As such, the chapter stresses the universality and everydayness of the control patterns depicted, laying the foundation for what follows. Chapters Two and Three increasingly zero in on the singles scene, specifying the dynamics of control that get unfortunately played out in and between people who self-consciously pursue an intimate connection with one another. The final chapter explores how issues of control affecting the person on the singles scene may be dealt with when he or she chooses to come to therapy.

In *The Singles Scene* and *The Puppeteers*, I offered every-day examples of various strategies or maneuvers by which people endeavor to covertly (and usually unconsciously) control other people. Although they were based on incidents reported by former patients of mine, they seemed to me to occur just as often to people who were not involved in therapy. At the time, I mentioned that the patterns of behavior depicted were only a handful in comparison with the thousands that were in use and I promised a more complete catalogue at a later date. The present volume is an attempt at such an exposition. As before, these examples, to my mind, are among the most prevalent and important. And as before, in each instance I typically begin with a brief clinical vignette that is interspersed or supplemented with a running commentary. Once again my hope is that their accumulated weight will make the theme of this book convincingly come to life.

1

Everyday Examples

GETTING REAL

Although there is virtually no limit to the variety of objects that people can nominate as sources of persecution, David was the first person I had met who genuinely felt harassed by a well-known radio talk show personality. In therapy, he regularly and vociferously chronicled the signature traits of that personality, all of which he found despicable. He was, first of all, rude to the very members of his audience foolhardy enough to accept his invitation to call in and freely express their views live on the air, frequently cutting them short, ridiculing their ideas, calling them names, or even hanging up on them. He was arrogant and extraordinarily opinionated. He presented himself as sufficiently informed on almost every current topic and judged people and events according to how well they accorded with his highly egocentric view of the world.

What most irked David, the reason he felt a prisoner of talk radio in his own home, was that his girlfriend, who frequently stayed over, was a devoted fan of this man and insisted on listening to him at every available opportunity. No amount of importuning could persuade her that the program was not only less than entertaining to him but an insult to his sensibilities. When I asked David why he thought his girlfriend so adored the same man he found so noxious, he blurted out, "Because she thinks he's so *real!*"

This was my personal introduction to the growing contemporary phenomenon of talk radio. Intrigued that some entertainment-driven invention of the media could stir such passion as to provoke considerable interpersonal discord, I listened, in the privacy of my home, for the first time to the man I had been hearing so much about in my office. And it did not take me long to realize that I wholeheartedly agreed with David's appraisal. The host was not merely offensive, he had elevated being offensive into an art. It was the display of personality not to please, but to shock. Most interesting to me—and once again I found myself in sync with my patient's perception—was the implicit claim that everything he said or did, no matter how vile, was somehow justified by the fact that, after all, he was only being real.

So what does it mean in today's world when a person is said to be, or is encouraged to be, real? When it is not used in the prescriptive mental health sense—referring to a person who may seem a trifle schizoid, out of touch, and in need of ego-psychological, adaptive reality-testing—it seems to imply:

1) On the cognitive level: that the person is in contact with the mainstream, consensually validated view of reality and therefore knows the relevant news stories, pop culture events, political issues, and everyday concerns of the average person of the social stratum to which he belongs;

2) On the psychological level: that there is a conjunction between what the person says and does, and what he says and means. Someone who is real is perceived as the antithesis of someone who is regarded as psychotic, that is, as someone who

lives, experiences, and reacts to the world of things and people as we know it. Such a person, for example, knows what day of the week, what season, what year it is. His perception of time and place, his orientation to what is immediately going on, has gone on, and seems about to go on will dovetail with our own. On the psychological level, therefore, such a person's behavior will fall within a range that is considered normal. A deviant response, for example, would be to answer (while busy doing something) someone who is politely inquiring if he can interrupt to ask a question, "Get out of my face!"; or to withdraw, as though from a palpable threat, from a passerby requesting the time; or to refuse—whether through a surplus of aggression or a dread of contact—to shake the hand of a stranger to whom one has been introduced.

Other than the perceptual, cognitive, and behavioral, there is another level by which people characteristically judge whether another person is real. This is the level of relationship, and it is the one that most interests us. By real, it is meant that there is a discernible congruence between what one says and does and what one says and means. Since to be real in the interpersonal realm—in the sense of unselfconsciously expressing one's actual self (Horney 1950) as opposed to one's ideal self—is exceedingly difficult, it is not surprising that most such endeavors fall considerably short of the mark. And what pass for authenticity, far more often than not (as in the case of the obstreperous radio host), are at bottom *ways of being pseudo-real*. For example:

1) By emphasizing for effect aspects of behavior associated with a lack of restraint: employing language, for example, that is colorful, risqué, or salty, or expressing emotions that are considered intemperate (offensively strong anger, outrageous opinions, unmitigated disgust, and so on). The message is that what

is underneath, unable to be held in check, has just broken out. People, therefore, will often try to act real by trying to appear unfinished, unintegrated, roughhewn, even self-contradictory. The unconscious equation they follow seems to be that what is genuine cannot be perfect, complete, or consistent.

2) By being, as a popular commercial warns against, "uncivilized": impolite or unsocial (as in burping, belching, yawning, groaning, or looking unkempt in the presence of others); unafraid or even relishing an occasional opportunity to appear ignorant (as in the classic "real" response to any portentous-sounding question, "I don't know"); or unashamedly emotive in situations where one is expected to be diplomatic (as in "What do I think of ——? I hate him!").

3) By shocking the other. Part of what is thought to be real is to be unpredictable. Since the litmus test of unpredictability is the register of surprise and the clearest evidence of surprise is the expression of shock, people who wish to impress others with how authentic they are will often go out of their way to produce dismay. For example: Q: "Who are you going to vote for in the upcoming presidential election?" A: "I'm not going to vote at all!"

4) By making a point of not hiding one's emotions even at the risk of coming across as intrusively demonstrative. Such a person who supposedly values being real will be unafraid to express what is happening to him even if he knows he will be offending others around him. For this reason, according to popular perception, to be real is to be true to one's self no matter what, to march to one's own drum, to be on one's own wavelength. And that is often equated with daring to be embarrassingly different: crying when it is considered unthinkable to cry, laughing when it is considered absurd to laugh. From that perspective, being real can mean being outrageously

or eccentrically individualistic, and popular movies shamelessly exploit this fact. (One of many examples is the film *Frankie and Johnny*, wherein Johnny—a recent ex-con who has learned that the way to happiness is to live according to one's own lights—realizing that he is hopelessly in love with Frankie—a woman who is frightened of her feelings—corners her in a crowded bowling alley and publicly asks her to be his wife and the mother of his children.)

5) By being stupid. Someone who is unafraid and unembarrassed to be thought of as (or to actually be) stupid, or worse, mentally defective—if that is what is required in order to honestly express oneself—by this logic is believed to be unquestionably genuine. And again the entertainment industry, as evidenced by blockbuster movies such as *Rain Man* and, especially, *Forrest Gump*, extolling people who seem to bask in their mental deficiency, capitalizes on this to the fullest.

6) By being a failure. In our society being a "loser," a marginal character, or an anti-hero is often perceived as testimony to the fact that sometimes, rather than don the mask of a false self in order to purchase success, a person would rather pay the price of failure (e. g., the movie *Barfly*, supposedly depicting the true-life story of a poet who existentially chooses a life of alcoholism and dereliction as a means of preserving his integrity).

7) By being a rebel. As proof of the urgency of the need to be true to oneself, a person may be willing to openly oppose an entire establishment that he regards as repressive.

8) By never lying even at the cost of being brutally honest. There is an illusion that to be real is to submit to a moral compulsion never to lie. In the past, radical groups such as the Black Muslims on the left and the John Birch Society on the right have adopted a purist stance of being unable to stomach the

prevailing hypocrisy of their time and then using that as a justification for indulging in behaviors that by conventional standards are flagrantly deviant.

9) By being politically incorrect. By the same logic, being what is called politically incorrect is seen as evidence of an untameable thirst to be real even at the risk of stepping on political toes.

10) By being criminal. For similar reasons, criminals are often seen, and artistically portrayed, as more honest than law-abiding citizens since they seem unafraid to give free reign to the occasional antisocial urges that most of us feel compelled to suppress.

11) By being insane. There is a long tradition in which the person whose ego has been irreparably shattered and who therefore cannot help but act out primal impulses shortly after they appear regardless of how out of touch with reality they are, is considered touchingly if pathetically true to his own mad self. Insanity, pathology, mental illness in greater or lesser degree are often viewed, in their self-destructive immediacy, as evidence of the power of the underlying raw psyche. And in the sense that being raw and unfinished is equated with real life, psychotic outbursts are often regarded as signs of a real, if sick, self.

12) By manifesting extreme physiological states. The behavior of people who are intoxicated, asleep, or comatose is considered real inasmuch as it appears at those times to have escaped the normal controls of the ego. When people begin to act as though their ego has been either overwhelmed (by irrepressible desires), broken down (by psychosis), or relegated to a secondary role (by being asleep), we are ready to assign to them the attribute "real."

13) By being in extreme pain. Since pain, physical or psychical, that crosses a certain critical threshold is thought to be incapable of being camouflaged, someone who appears visibly distressed is generally given the benefit of the doubt and believed. We do not doubt the authenticity of the person who has been knocked down by an automobile and is moaning in the street, or who looks ashen as he lies on an operating table waiting to be wheeled into major surgery, or who cries out in anguish for help after discovering that his wallet has just been stolen.

14) By being moody. Inasmuch as a mood is considered to be an internal state of mind so pressing that it temporarily dominates the consciousness of the person (Bollas 1987), its authenticity is usually not questioned and this is especially true if someone happens to be in a bad mood. So while it is commonplace to suspect that an individual may be reacting in a disingenuous fashion, it is rare to actually accuse someone of simulating an entire mood (if only because to do so could tax the energies of even a gifted actor).

15) By being angry or enraged. Again, because the direct expression of anger or rage is so frowned upon in our culture, where being in control or "cool" is more and more the vogue, that its occurrence tends not only not to be doubted, but is often memorialized: "I always thought he had a pleasant disposition, but can you ever forget that time he lost it!"

If it is true, as I believe, that all of the above are examples of being only pseudo-real, the question arises as to why the genuine article is so hard to find. Part of the answer may be that the popular conception of what counts as being real hinges on issues of control versus loss of control. Because the contemporary mind so believes in the necessity of control to survive in the high-tech, overspecialized, and super-competitive world, the loss or breakdown of such control is inevitably magnified and accorded a spurious stature: it is labelled *real*.

From this standpoint, someone who is *real* is someone who is exposing the nitty-gritty, the underbelly, the psychic stuff that lies beneath the elaborate armor of defensive control that each of us is obliged to don at the start of each day. A corollary of this is that such bottom-line personality traits are most likely to emerge under moments of unusual stress, or internal damage to or relaxation of everyday adaptive mechanisms of control.

Although there is more than a kernel of truth to this conception of the real as something that only peeps through when the control apparatus fails, it is, nevertheless, a romanticization. By contrast, there is a long tradition of psychodynamic and psychoanalytic thinkers such as Karen Horney (1950), with her emphasis on the actual or real self as opposed to the ideal self, D. W. Winnicott (1960), with his seminal concept of the true and the false self, and Christopher Bollas (1992), with his representation of the simple and complex self, who view the real as an intricate interpersonal and object-relational achievement. Instead of being a mere photocopy of what is inside someone or a transfer of psychic information, from the standpoint of intimate human relations the *real* is an act of transformation. In *Portrait of the Artist as a Young Patient* (Alper 1992), I explored some of the imaginary components of what is customarily thought to be real and suggested that without such a creative transformation of the elements of one's self in a given moment of interpersonal time, there can be no meaningful revelation of what is uniquely human and real.

If the real involves expression, affirmation, and symbolization and is not a simple, behavioral, or informational X-ray of what is normally concealed, it follows that it will occur only rarely. Someone who genuinely appreciates what is real about another will intuitively understand that the attribution does not refer to the unchanging bedrock of a personality, but to a dynamic quality that to a large measure is dependent on how much one trusts the relationship at hand. Thus, for example, if someone harbors a component of "real" anger toward a person one does not trust, the relationship can go on for years or even forever without the true anger being revealed (a common scenario with which every therapist is familiar).

It is therefore not a case of just observing what is authentic in the other, but of being able and motivated to facilitate it. Such a facilitator is someone who understands that trust must be established first; that what is real about the other is in a sense the most precious thing a person can give and therefore is something not to be idly surveyed, but cultivated; that it cannot be taken in without empathy and imagination; and, finally, that the real requires in turn a real response that always entails some effort.

On the one hand, a person who reveals his true self is taking a risk that whatever is most important to him may be rejected. On the other hand, to respond and resonate with what is real in another is to accept an invitation to draw a little closer, become a little more intimate, and to explore a little more adventurously the possibilities of self-other interrelating—which is no less of a risk.

By contrast, the need for the pseudo-real is an attempt not only to avoid such risks, but to control them: the wish to have someone act or be superficially real is a means people use to reassure themselves that they have nothing to be afraid of, gratify their voyeurism, and (perhaps most common) to be entertained. If it is remembered that people who are cynical, rude, aggressive, hedonistic, frankly opportunistic, or self-proclaimed rogues—the stock-in-trade characters of TV and daily soaps—are typically regarded as real, it can be understood why they are also considered entertaining (provided, of course, they operate at a safe remove and do not stir up too much anxiety). The connection is not trivial. If it is true that the litmus test

for the creditability of self-expression is either the dissolving
or surmounting of the normal civilizing constraints of the self
so that something more spontaneous, animated, and unfettered
can break free, then its natural occurrence can easily be vicari-
ously enjoyed as a kind of brief serendipitous stimulation that
leavens the tedium of everyday life.

If, however, a pressure or expectation to be real develops
that is in the service of a defensive need to be reassured, gratified, or entertained, it will have little to do with intimacy. On
some level the other will know this and experience being "real"
in this sense as, basically, being merely compliant. A classic
American example is the nearly ubiquitous, unspoken demand
to smile in a variety of social contexts that are similar only in
their discomfort: meeting someone one does not particularly
want to meet for the first time; having to impress a superior,
such as one's boss, that one is in command of a situation that
one secretly fears one is actually losing control of; considering
oneself obligated to act like a happy person in spite of the fact
that one feels insecure, anxious, depressed, demoralized, and
completely unsocial. When such is the case, the requirement
to smile is a form of social control and the behavioral simulation of the state of mind of a person who seemingly is content
and in possession of good mental health is at best a compliant
facade.

From this perspective, the enormous interpersonal pressure
that is brought to bear on the other to be what is commonly
called real can be a covert desire for avoidance of genuine contact. In its stead is an attempt to create an artificial relationship
with a pseudo-real person: someone who is sufficiently upfront
and unambiguous about what he or she is feeling, thinking, and
doing so as to provide the required reassurance that the presence confronting one is not a mysterious thing, necessitating a
potentially risky exploration in order to know it.

To sum up: the demand to model oneself in conformance to a false but pleasing psychic reality is at bottom an interpersonal strategy meant to strike a homeostatic balance between authentic contact that frightens one because it is too intimate and too real and manifest alienation that disturbs one because it is too hostile and indifferent. Fed by twin fears, the pressure to be safely real is, therefore, an underrated but powerful control game.

TAMING OF THE SHREW

Complaining is such a universal component of the process of psychotherapy that it passes largely unnoticed and, indeed, to talk about complaining can itself seem a form of complaining. Yet there is hardly a session in which some deep-seated complaint, vocal or muted, explicit or hidden, honestly owned or disingenuously projected, is not bitterly lodged. Although I knew nearly all patients do it, it was Richard who taught me that complaining, when raised to an art, could be virtually toxic. Of course, in spite of the fact that he railed endlessly in his sessions against the woman with whom he lived, he did not conceive of himself as a complainer. It was Marcia, with her morning litany of grievances that she unfailingly recited, who was the gadfly in the relationship.

Why even before the sleep was rubbed out of her eyes, while still propped on an elbow as she gathered her strength to raise herself from bed and begin her day, her face would be furrowed in a complaining look. "What is it? You look worried." Finding the bait irresistible, Richard could not help but cautiously inquire, hoping against hope that he had misread her mood.

"It's nothing new. I have writing and heartache." She meant finishing the interminable treatment reports (which she despised) that were expected of her as a supervisor in a social services agency, and then girding herself to face the inevitable frustrations that seemed to forever haunt her private universe.

Richard's frustration with Marcia's frustration was made more acute by the fact that when she wasn't complaining, when she wasn't setting her jaw, grinding her teeth, or pouting at her world (at which time he felt he was engaged in a modern version of the taming of the shrew), she was capable of a blend of sweetness and loving nurturance he had never before experienced.

With Richard, therefore, I was able to observe the corrosive dynamics of the art of complaining with a clarity that up until that point had eluded me. A complaint, I began to realize, effectively controls the behavior of the other because it externalizes the source of the pain while simultaneously conferring the identity of victim: the message is sent that the complainer is in no way the author of the torment she is harboring. Not only that, but the responsibility for the person's suffering is typically projected upon the other, who is accused of being the sole guilty party.

Because a complaint can seem like such a no-win situation for the target at whom it is directed, it cannot help but engender resentment. One essentially is left with two markedly poor choices: either to contest the authenticity of the accusation, which usually inspires the complainant to litigate her grievances that now include the new one of the other being shamefully unempathic, or to compromise oneself by validating an allegation one consciously does not believe in or one unconsciously chooses to embrace through a defensive process of identification with the aggressor.

To the degree that the accusation of wrongdoing is personalized, it becomes divisive. The recipient knows that empathy has now gone out the window and his only choice is to decide whether or not to relate to the complaint that becomes more and more solipsistic, taking on a life of its own and drawing the brunt of attention to itself. It is not uncommon therefore for the recipient to sit helplessly by and gradually begin to feel envious of or competitive with a complaint that has become the focus of the interaction.

A complaint, therefore, is an urgent signal, an SOS, that something comparable to a physical injury has occurred on the emotional, psychological plane. An unmitigated insult to the psyche has been registered that cries out for remediation. The implication is that there is nothing more important in the world at this dynamic moment in time than to meet the allegation head on. For someone, however, who is being directly accused or held partly responsible for the other's publicized suffering it is difficult not to feel immediately defensive. To the recipient the complaint typically sounds like a demand for punitive damages. A further implication is that the alleged abuse has been repetitive, obvious in nature, and, therefore, that compensation is long overdue. But since the putative defendant almost invariably thinks that the grievances have been overrated and that his behavior could not possibly have been as persecutory as is being claimed, he will naturally resent the aura of urgency that is attached to the complaint and believe that what is needed instead is space and time to adjudicate how the complainant arrived at her peculiarly agonized state of mind. To the complainant, however, such an attitude will be viewed as a tactic designed to postpone taking responsible action and further proof of just what the person has had to put up with.

To the other, the plea for almost instant change can only seem dictatorial and it will not be long before—as more and more he realizes that his own autonomous input into the situation is regarded as not only irrelevant but as intrusive—he perhaps perceives himself as the one who is being persecuted by the persistent and strident charge that he is somehow persecuting the other.

Such repetition is a cardinal characteristic of the interpersonal complaint and is probably the thing the auditor finds most unbearable and punishing to be subjected to. It is as though the complaining person, who usually feels she has suffered in silence too long, is determined to go public with the history of her abuse and to stay public until something has been done about it. Thus, compulsive reiteration, which is born of the hopelessness that there is anyone out there who really cares, is a necessary part of the presentation of most complaints. To the accused, however, who generally sees himself as fundamentally or at least partially innocent of the allegations he is charged with, this repetition can only seem like punitive redundancy.

For all of these reasons, someone who complains is often viewed as profoundly narcissistic and it is therefore not surprising that the compensation being demanded is typically to be distributed to only one person. From the perspective of the other, the complaint feels like extortion. Almost never does a person to whom a complaint is directed think that he is being respected, if only because the tone in which it is couched is characteristically badgering and it is therefore easy to wonder if the hectoring itself is intended as a punishment in advance for the alleged mistreatment.

From the standpoint of the one who is issuing the complaint, however, there is a sense in which the steady pressure put on the other to make amends is unconsciously aimed at recreating in that person a type of recurrent abuse analogous to the experience constituting the original complaint. If the intention is really to coerce reparation by inflicting a sobering lesson, the complaint is self-defeating because it cannot help but provoke resistance in the other who rightly perceives the badgering as a wish to punish rather than a desire to set things right. The complainant often foresees this and, regarding it as one more proof she will not be attended to, escalates the demand. In this way, a complaint can very quickly become a form of desperate blackmail: the threat, inherent in the maddening reiteration, like a wailing siren that won't stop, that unless it gets its way, it will continue to clamorously and intrusively make itself heard.

A complaint may be an attempt to utilize the capacity of pain to be disruptive. Something that won't go away will be attended to, even if negatively so. Furthermore, underlying the urgent impulse to externalize and act out inner pain may be a secret wish to achieve a belated communication by fostering a symbiosis of abuse and a parity of victimization.

Undeniably there is also retaliation at work—as though the complainant is saying, "If you are going to insist on *not* hearing me, I am going to insist that you do" (and at this point, it is indistinguishable from a power struggle).

Of course, a complaint can be levied with tact and respect, in the service of working things out, but this, as every therapist knows, is rather rare. Far more often, the intent is to disturb the peace of mind of the auditor with the threatening message that unless she is at least minimally pacified, no different kind of interaction will take place. From the interpersonal standpoint, the delivery of a complaint is therefore tantamount to a relational strike. Compounding this is that the other knows that the last thing the striker now has on her mind is his needs, inasmuch as he apparently is presumed to be both in control and responsible for her miseries.

Understandably, he will feel profoundly abandoned by the complainant. He realizes his only hope of being recognized as a person in his own right with needs of his own is to first attend to the grievances of the other, but since he usually feels his solicitude is being unfairly coerced, his first instinct will be to attack his accuser, which he intuitively recognizes will only make matters worse. His choices therefore shrink to submitting to the indictment (nolo contendere) or to escalating the fray by pleading his innocence.

Since both choices are decidedly poor, there is unavoidable tension and anxiety preoccupying both parties who, more and more, try to jockey for position in the ensuing power play. Purely from the vantage point of minimizing the interpersonal options of the other—luring him or her into a stance of either frustrating compliance or combative alienation—complaining is a powerful control game.

BEING STUBBORN

Arthur, a pleasant-looking, large man, who works as an assistant to a well-known modern artist, is recounting an argument he has had with Michael, a contractor. It seems everything is in dispute: the price, the time of delivery, the quantity of the order. On every point, hotly debated over a period of hours, Arthur is certain he is right. The only thing he is really interested in exploring in therapy are the motives underlying Michael's peculiar refusal to accept the truth. It does not occur to Arthur that there is something at least equally "peculiar" in the unclouded vision he somehow always manages to achieve on every feature of a disagreement, no matter how complicated. Nor is he puzzled by the fact that the people who know him, professionally and socially, with few exceptions are united in their reluctance to enter into an argument with him. Indeed, he understands that his characteristic level-headed objectivity, as he sees it, turns most people off. What he does not grasp, however, is how to deal with the disturbing subjectivity of someone who does not realize he is being subjective.

It is in the nature of being stubborn not to admit that one is being stubborn, and in this regard Arthur is similar to every other stubborn patient I've ever worked with. There are as many ways to be divisive as there are people, but being stubborn must be one of the most efficient. Analogous to the person who insistently voices a complaint, a stubborn person seemingly draws a line in the sand, indicating that the forward motion of the interaction has just come to a grinding halt. Whatever happens now will be retrospective or revisionist in that it will attempt to settle what is now considered to be urgent unfinished business. The message is, "No, you don't!" and the metamessage is, "I will pursue this to the bitter end and do what is necessary to prevail."

To the other, such diehard resistance can only be frightening. No matter how forewarned one was of the person's recalcitrant temperament, the stubbornness is usually perceived as a surprising example of resistive overkill. The experience is akin to encountering someone who, for one reason or another, is intent to a bizarre degree on holding on to what seems an ordinary dynamic moment in interpersonal time. Stubbornness can therefore be regarded as the antithesis of letting go, which is the hallmark of intimacy. It is as though the stubborn individual has made a grudge-like promise to himself to nip in the bud at any cost a potentially unbearable offense. From that standpoint, interpersonal time metaphorically seems to stop and to the other the interaction can begin to proceed in agonizing slow motion, having become now the adversarial relationship par excellence. (One is reminded here of Harry Stack Sullivan's [1953] wonderful phrase, "the flypaper technique," used to describe the uncanny way obsessively resistive people shadow their adversary's every move and refuse to be shaken from their purpose.)

Someone who is openly stubborn is thereby intimidating because he seems to have so much more energy than you do at his disposal—as does the person who grows unexpectedly enraged or who suddenly complains—on the particular sticking point. And it is therefore difficult to believe you can hold your own, let alone make a meaningful, personal impact. Not surprisingly, a typical initial response to a display of stubbornness in the other is a mixture of anger and discouragement. The person has gotten so worked up at what seemingly is an ordinary detail in the interactional flux that one realizes that any plausible hope for an interpersonal context to develop, in which serious thoughts, feelings, and impressions can be both differentiated and integrated, has effectively vanished. Instead, there is a lopsided emphasis on what the person has become fixated on, which to the other can only be experienced as obsessive resistance.

Characterologically, stubbornness tends to be passive-aggressive, defensive, and resistive. The anger and aggression that usually are at the core of the need to be stubborn are often expressed through the successful frustration of the other's aims. The recalcitrant person has no interest in the interpersonal future, no wish to negotiate or collaborate in the present towards the implementation of a mutual, if not immediately attainable, goal. On the contrary, what he wants to do above all is to bring what he considers an oppressive state of affairs to a grinding and instant halt. He wants *negative closure*. In no small part, therefore, it is this perception of the lack of an interpersonal future that is so disheartening to the target of the oppositionalism.

No one, of course, is as hopeless as the stubborn person, whose stubbornness grows out of a deep pessimism that anyone would voluntarily give him what he needs and whose only recourse therefore is to engage in a bitter fight for survival. Such cynicism cannot help but be apparent to the other, and is a further cause for distance and alienation. Someone who opposes another in this way, seeing little of human kindness, empathy, or nurturance, regarding the other as essentially a suppressive, malign agency that desperately needs to be thwarted, automatically dehumanizes the object of his scorn. Rightly, the individual feels reduced to an impersonal force and from a dynamic interpersonal standpoint, the acting out of stubborn intentionality will easily dissipate into a contest of naked wills. It will then be experienced, as are all profoundly non-intimate interactions, as meaningless.

In effect, the person who begins to stubbornly oppose invites the other to follow him down an interpersonal blind alley. It is the dread of so doing that makes it such a powerful, albeit primitive, control game.

PRESUMED INNOCENT

Judy is a petite, animated woman who seems to thrive on the pressures that go along with being a successful copywriter in a prosperous advertising agency. As she sees it, she has only a single problem, which, however, is two-pronged: on the one hand she finds herself incapable of agreeing with almost anything anyone says to her and thus is ready to debate at the drop of a pin, and on the other she takes wicked pleasure in using her formidable oratorical talents to not only outshine but to demolish her hand-picked opponents. Although she combines, from the standpoint of interrelating, some of the more problematic characteristics of oppositionalism and argumentativeness, she acts blissfully unaware of the searing impact her contentiousness has on others, and wants only to understand why people get so mad at her.

Judy realizes she is an extraordinary debater, and was so well before she received official recognition as the undisputable star performer of her college debating team. As a teenager, she would regularly express her anger to her mother, not by fighting with her, but by debating her. And these were debates, not arguments. Much as her mother, a sensitive, level-headed, and somewhat taciturn woman, loathed them, she was unable to avoid being lured into them. When they were over, she did not feel so much defeated by her daughter as utterly humiliated by her.

As Judy would chronicle in her sessions the cause of these debates past and present (and especially their aftermath), a pattern emerged. Because she was such a natural and unconscious expert at setting up and springing her litigious traps on unsuspecting victims, I was able to see just how effective the art of debating can be as a means of controlling the behavior of the other. Of course, few people can really debate well and what starts out as a debate will often quickly degenerate into an argument, at which people are probably even less adept. The difficulty in decisively winning a debate, however, has hardly proved a deterrent to entering into one and this, I suggest, is partly because it seemingly offers a tantalizing strategy for controlling the other.

I happen to be writing this in the midst of the media feeding frenzy that has been triggered by the O. J. Simpson trial. I cannot help but note that what I have to say about the tendency to debate—how it controls the other by establishing an irrevocable, non-intimate relationship—is perfectly encapsulated in the adversarial legal system, especially the one that deals with criminal offenses. As I can think of no better example than this, it may be useful to digress and examine, from a purely psychodynamic perspective, just what the daily televised court proceedings of the so-called "trial of the century" are really revealing to the nation.

TRIAL BY JURY

Each side is allowed to be as biased as possible. Once charges have been pressed, and even before the trial has begun, both prosecution and defense are expected to have completely committed themselves to one side of the truth. When the trial begins they are permitted within the limits of law, as arbitrated by the judge, to employ every imaginable strategy to obtain the verdict they want. From that point on, once the system has been set in motion, it is understood that there will be no negotiation, reconsideration, or dynamic interchange of viewpoints. Short of changing a plea due to unforeseen exigencies in the course of the trial, it is unheard of for either side to retreat or especially to switch from the position originally marked out.

So both sides press on and the only real issue in doubt is who is going to win, to be strictly determined by whether the trial results in a conviction or acquittal. Looked at in this way, it very much resembles a contest or juridical game, but one that relies on strategic moves rather than on human interaction. Under the ideological justification that it is better to have rule by law rather than by people—that it is better or safer to be governed by abstract principles of justice than be subject to the vicissitudes of subjective human judgment—an elaborate, impersonal machinery has evolved, a cardinal characteristic of which is that it must remain impervious to the dynamic changes and relevant information that arise in the instantaneous present. Everything that occurs is to be referred backwards to a series of casebook laws that were created in the distant past but will exert complete control (until and unless amended) over what happens in either the immediate present or foreseeable future. From an interpersonal, dynamic perspective in which empathy, mutuality, and intersubjectivity are prime movers, such a system is effectively *dead*: the outcome of what happens between people is regulated by rules rather than by psyches.

When that happens, and as the rules begin systematically to be applied, the system can only detach itself from its creators and quickly assume a life of its own. What was after all originally designed to be a servant of people instead becomes their master. This may be why in the trial of O. J. Simpson there was a sense in which all of the participants, from the defendant to the witnesses, the defense "dream team," righteous prosecutors, and impervious judge, were ultimately puppets.

If it is true that all of the human agents are dwarfed by the system that envelops them, this may explain why the issue of bias or untoward influence is such a crucial one. If everyone is in the grip of something external and impersonal, it is understandable that an oppositional desire will arise to restore oneself by exerting as much human control (or bias) wherever it is possible. What this comes down to is an often desperate attempt to assert one's will in a system that is dominated by rules and laws. In terms of Leslie Farber's (1976) concept of trying to will what cannot be willed and control what cannot be controlled, such an attempt is impossible and, not surprisingly, can result in morbid, even paranoid, sensitivity to the other's bias: if one is indeed only a puppet controlled by a labyrinthine bureaucratic machinery, then no one else must be allowed to covertly seize any reins of power to which they are not entitled. Ironically, this leads both sides to do their utmost to ensure that the jury is free of bias. (This, at bottom, is a displacement of a frustrated need to deny bias or influence to the system and to their opponent.)

From our psychodynamic perspective, it is significant that in the eyes of the law, the *psyches* of its key officers, the prosecutor, defense counsel, and judge, do not count so long as the rules are being adhered to and there is no overt disturbance of the procedural flow. When that is the case, then even if the prosecutor or defense attorney is secretly irrational, pathological, or criminal, it will not matter. What does matter is the outcome of the predetermined clash of two opposing wills, the prosecution and the defense, out of which something euphemistically called the truth is supposed to emerge.

In actuality, however, the legal system will often reveal who is a better debater and not who has discovered the greater truth. Analogous to two prize fighters, the one left standing who is declared the winner may indeed be the better survivor and the more immune to attack, but not necessarily the one who has more wisdom. It may be, therefore, that the justice system has confused adversarial competition and obsessional doubting with the discovery of truth. An original fear of being controlled may have given rise to an obsessional desire to create a level playing field; obsessional doubts as to whether it is possible to receive a fair and impartial trial may have led to the institutionalization of a fierce adversarial system that fosters the relentless devaluation of the opposing viewpoint.

I think it is revealing to ask oneself whether there has ever been a time when an important personal decision—one that required objectivity, fair-mindedness, sound judgment, and extensive life experience—was made on the basis of the trial-by-jury system. For the overwhelming majority of people, the answer must be no.

While there may be open-mindedness in the natural process of productively rendering a decision or discovering a personal truth, there is definitely not a savage point and counterpoint for every issue raised. Instead, sooner or later, a predominant viewpoint will crystallize which then may be subjected to careful scrutiny for possible error.

The analogue in science to this process of skeptical decision making, supposedly in the service of discovering the truth, is experimental verification. The crucial difference, however, is that in a legitimately honest, scientific search for truth, experimentation is used in the spirit of openness and sincere hope to find the truth. The potentially falsifying experiment is employed as a safety check and not as an instrument of devaluation.

In the trial-by-jury system, the originally democratic and scientific model has been perverted into a search-and-destroy mission wherein each side fights to demolish the validity of the other. In practice this means that the prosecution in order to maximize their aggressive potential, will often overindict a defendant, while the defense, under the shibboleth of reasonable doubt, will attempt to becloud and confuse every imaginable issue.

At the root of the trial-by-jury system, I believe, is a profound lack of trust on the part of the ordinary person that anyone can ever, especially in a time of crisis, be genuinely and empathically fair to him. What this means is that the only way that one can vindicate oneself when legally charged with serious misconduct is by emerging victorious from an all-or-nothing power struggle, which in turn means incessantly undermining the opposing side. This original, universal, profound skepticism of the ability to receive a truly fair trial is then projected upon the formation of an abstract jury system. Over the course of time, because of this underlying, deep-seated mistrust, the search for truth has often been institutionally degraded to only a struggle and process of obsessional, albeit juridical, doubting. The side that is left standing and least scathed at the end (i. e., that secures the verdict it has fought for) is judged to be the one that is most worthwhile and is therefore the one that is settled for. From that standpoint, the dynamics of a trial by jury are analogous to those of a conflicted individual who, weary of an internal obsessional debate over what is the correct course of action on a complicated issue, may finally embrace the opinion that has best survived the attrition of a seemingly endless inner cross-examination.

Although the clash of wills between the prosecution and the defense is typically viewed as a democratic process or competition in which the proverbial best man or woman is supposed to win, it is scarcely the same kind of competition sponsored by the free enterprise system or seen in the sporting arena in which both winner and loser are supposed to benefit. If it is a contest, it is an *adversarial* one, in which the success of one participant results in the failure of the other. Another way to put this is to say that it is a zero-sum contest: somebody wins and somebody loses. Obviously people know this and realize that the consequences of a trial by jury in a criminal case are prodigious. And should a miscarriage of justice occur—as must occasionally happen in even the best judicial system—then the consequences are even more prodigious: either innocent men or women are convicted of crimes they didn't commit and deprived of fundamental human liberties, or dangerous and guilty criminals are acquitted and allowed to continue to prey on an unsuspecting society.

If the legal system is adversarial, it may be helpful, in order to understand its present-day enormous sophistication and complexity, to apply to it the concept of an explosive arms race. Originally used to describe the escalating effects of a nuclear arms race between nations, the concept has been borrowed by biologists to explain the evolutionary development over great stretches of time of increasingly sophisticated weapons of offense and defense among predators (e.g., lions) and their prey (e.g., gazelles).

Now, the whole point of an explosive arms race, when it occurs among animals, is that as one side gets better, so does the other: the better the lion gets at catching the gazelle, the faster the gazelle runs. The reason improvement on one side is matched by counterimprovements on the other side, as determined in this case by natural selection, is that each side *must* improve in order not to die out.

The ironic conclusion of all this, however, as Richard Dawkins (1986) brilliantly points out in *The Blind Watchmaker*, is that, although the lion of today is better equipped to hunt the gazelle of today than the lion of a million years ago and although the gazelle of today is equally better equipped to evade the lion than the gazelle of a million years ago, neither is necessarily more *successful* at it. In other words, if every improvement on one side is matched by a neutralizing improvement on the other side, the *rate* of success today may not actually be better than it was a million years ago.

Which is why, as has often been noted, what explosive arms races really accomplish is only to stalemate one another. Since, however, the cost to both sides of producing the end-result stalemate is tremendous, the question arises: Why bother to join in an arms race in the first place? And the answer is that once one side starts it, the other cannot afford not to join in. Thus, once an animal such as a lion suddenly, as a result of natural selection, begins to invest more than its customary resources in catching its customary prey, the gazelle, in order not to be driven into extinction, must keep pace.

Analogously, once a nation such as the United States develops a nuclear warhead, another nation such as Russia cannot afford not to develop a defensive missile. And once a defensive missile that is superior to our warhead has been produced, we cannot afford not to counter that with a weapon that is better than its predecessor, and so on. The reason, therefore, that the term *explosive* or *runaway* is applied to an arms race (whether between nations, people, or animals) is that it exemplifies what happens when a process of positive feedback goes unchecked. Such a process is comparatively rare. We are much more familiar with cases of negative feedback, which operates, for example, in a thermostat and in many systems of the human body and is essentially corrective and self-monitoring. By contrast, positive feedback feeds off itself: each chain in the link, in effect, is a green light signaling the next link to go ahead but at a faster pace—the classic example being nuclear fission.

If the O. J. Simpson trial has truly demonstrated anything to the American public, it is how incredibly sophisticated the prosecution and defense were when it came to canceling one another out. If, as I suggest, what we really saw was not a glorious lesson in how efficiently the justice system works, but the ironic end result of an explosive arms race between the prosecution and the defense that has been going on for hundreds of years, the question arises: How and why did this happen?

The answer, in no small measure, lies in the confusion between the democratic and competitive American way of life, in which everyone is supposedly given an equal opportunity to excel or to win, and the adversarial contest, in which there is to be only one winner and one loser. First of all, at least theoretically, justice is supposed to be for everyone: for the people and for the defendant. Justice for the people means that the individual who unlawfully and destructively preys upon them shall be held accountable and restrained for as long as is necessary. Justice for the defendant means he shall not be held accountable or have to answer to any charges that are based on crimes he did not commit. Justice for the defendant, of course, does not mean he shall be acquitted of a crime he committed. Instead, justice for the defendant, whose guilt has been proven beyond reasonable doubt, means he shall be held accountable by being incarcerated in a penal institution where not only society shall be safe from him, but where he will be safe from his own self-destructive tendencies, that is, safe from endangering himself by committing an even greater crime in the future and thereby at least granted the time in which to rehabilitate himself.

Juridical pieties aside, few really believe that justice is equally and fairly distributed to both the people and the defendant. An important reason is that laws that are enacted to bring criminals to justice are, in general, patently punitive. By punitive I mean excessively and unfairly punishing. This is because such laws are governmental expressions of the anger that you or I would feel if seriously threatened by a dangerous criminal. From a psychodynamic standpoint, it might be said that the penal code is based on fantasies of retaliation rather than on personal experience (since it is safe to assume that the majority of lawmakers were not crime victims) and then justified by referring to the abstract history of English law, which may or may not have had any direct relevancy to everyday life.

If it is true that the penal code to a large extent is excessively punitive, it follows that the isolated individual who finds himself charged by the state with a very serious crime will tend to feel persecuted. Thus, right from the start, an unfortunate dynamic gets set up. The defendant and his attorney typically feel they are being unfairly ganged up on by the generally superior people's prosecutorial team and they often respond by overreacting: in this case by overdefending—aggressively searching for ways to drastically reduce the charges that have been levied, even if it means allowing a guilty man to be acquitted because of a technicality. The prosecution, seeing that the defense is overreacting by overdefending, characteristically counters by overcharging: asking for a hundred years of prison time in the hope of getting at least twenty.

From the inception of the legal system in this country, and abetted by an increasingly precise technology, the prosecution has steadily gotten better. But so has the defense, who, in order to keep pace, has relied more and more on loopholes in the law, not to speak of its own battery of opposing forensic experts. The result has been an explosive arms race between prosecution and defense personified by the "trial of the century" in which, regardless of the verdict, the two sides seemed so evenly matched.

Finally, in their effort to deny their sense of imprisonment within the bureaucratic machinery of the justice system, the chief officers of the court (prosecutor, defense attorney and judge) will often attempt to assert their will at the expense of the jury. Thus, the jury is commanded to obey the almost impossible injunction to uphold the presumption of innocence in the face of the antithetical assumption by the court of near total guilt as evidenced by the incarceration of the defendant and (if deemed appropriate) refusal of bail. On the one hand, the jury is appointed to be the ultimate arbiter of facts; on the other, they are meticulously instructed in the law. They are told what they can hear and what they cannot. They are presented with the exact criteria by which they are to make their decision. They are often sequestered and placed under guard.

They are presented with the rationale that in order to arrive at an impartial and objective decision, they must be as free of biases as possible. Indeed, the only biases they are allowed to be subjected to are those of the prosecution and the defense, both of whom are permitted by law to passionately advocate their favorite theory of the crime.

Somehow, out of this contest between an admittedly and completely biased prosecutor and defense attorney, as refereed by a supposedly fair-minded judge, something called the truth is presumed to emerge.

From a psychodynamic perspective, the recondite and ponderous machinery of the legal system can be viewed as an institutional denial of underlying feelings of emasculation when it comes to the prevention of serious criminal acts and a retroactive attempt to make reparation and to partially undo the crime which it is trying. Seen in this light, salient characteristics of the legal system—its incredible thoroughness, overwhelming slowness, hair-splitting precision, government by rules and abstract principles, absolute refusal to be influenced by anything other than juristic logic—are exhibitionistic, grandiose denials of the very features that denote the crime it is trying: irrationality, impulsivity, and profound disregard for the consequences of one's actions. This becomes especially clear when one compares the behavior of the criminal with that of the court that tries him. Even when premeditated, criminal acts tend to be poorly planned, executed in haste, and revelatory of impaired foresight. By contrast, the legal system moves at a tortoise's pace, obsesses over almost every detail, and lays unnatural emphasis upon logical consistency. Its goal appears to be the enactment of purely abstract principles of human behavior as opposed to the kind of animalistic submission to

anti-social urges that result in crimes of violence, and, by such
an awesome, terrifying, and punitive display of inhuman self-
control, it seeks to deny that it is essentially unable to implement much of what it was originally set up to do: prevent acts
of crime, serve as an efficient role model for the citizenry as
to how justice should be served, and thereby, by the trickle-
down effect, influence and improve the conduct of human
affairs.

On a much less grandiose scale, there is the formal debate
and, on the plane of everyday experience, there is the universal tendency to become, under moments of stress, argumenta-
tive, both of which incorporate many of the above characteristics. A debate, for example, is similar to a courtroom trial:

1) It is clearly adversarial. It reduces the act of conversation to a contest, in which the winner is supposed to be the
best debater.

2) It is completely rule-bound. Other than the manipulation
of the rules, which is largely left up to the spontaneity and
ingenuity of the participants, the principal agenda has been
set well in advance.

3) The participants are not free to react to each other out
of their personal center, autonomously expressing and sharing
thoughts, feelings, and impressions, but must use the response
of their opponent as the primary input, which is to be processed
according to predetermined guidelines. In a debate, therefore,
the key determinants of the behavior of the participants and
the eventual outcome of the debate itself are, first, the rules
that are in force and, second, the specific level of skill of the
participants.

What such a conception of the justice system and a debate
leaves out, of course, are the *psyches* of the players. It therefore tends to be overlooked that even if principles, rules, and

skill are to be what drives the course of events, their application must always be mediated by psyches. And from the standpoint of interpersonal intimacy, this has dire consequences. It means that nothing spontaneous, creative, or genuine, however meaningful, that lies outside the designated constraints will be tolerated. Because a game tends to draw a person more and more into its world—it is easy to become obsessed with or hooked on the ingenious strategies available to the expert game player—it is commonplace to disregard everything a game, or game-like interaction, leaves out. One cannot, for example, change the rules, invent new ones, or negotiate the rules, and one certainly cannot ignore them.

In contrast to the rules of a game, which are arbitrary, the rules of the legal system are supposedly grounded in sound experience pertaining to the practice of establishing necessary social restraints. In this sense, they are supposed to be somewhat like the customs and mores (e. g., be civil to strangers) that society creates in order to regulate and facilitate the interactive flux of human behavior. A crucial difference, of course, is that social mores are subject to individual judgments, human needs, and especially to immediate feedback, and to that extent are modifiable.

Since, however, the rules of law and of a debate are not affected by the passage of time per se, they are impervious to whatever present pain their enactment may be causing a particular person. Although the rules often contain within themselves a subset of rules designed to permit amendment in the event of serious transgressions or miscarriages of the original rules, this can only take place in the future. In other words, rules are blind, deaf, and dumb to the present. They tend to live conservatively in the past when they were created or in the future where they are speculatively open to revision. While their effects are very much felt in the present, therefore, they themselves or, more specifically, what they represent, does not dynamically change.

A trial by jury or even a formalized debate of supposedly national importance (e. g., a presidential one), while often highly dramatic because of the obvious consequences its outcome is sure to have for certain people, can in itself be curiously devoid of meaning or genuine passion. While active involvement in either can regularly elicit intense feelings in the participants and on occasion engender an adversarial, negative bonding (based on a profound, symbiotic mistrust), it does not typically result in a nurturing relationship.

If a trial by jury can be looked upon as a governmentally legitimized debate, and if a debate between two parties can be looked upon as a formalized argument, then it may be seen how effective they are as a means for avoiding intimacy.

In this regard, it is revealing to observe two people who begin to lose control and to engage in a heated argument. Although the fine art of persuasion cherished by lawyers and debaters alike may be nowhere in sight, they nevertheless may manage to sound like and to employ many of the tactics, however clumsily, of the professional advocate.

In short, human objectivity is not a dry exercise in how to use the principles of formal logic. It is instead an end product and composite of a conscientious, empathic self-restraint born of a nurturing desire to respect the boundaries of the other and a passionate investment of one's true self in the issue at hand.

From the psychodynamic standpoint, interpersonal truth, if it is to exist, is something that can only emerge from the creative and dynamic interplay between self and other.

"I HAVE SOMETHING TO TELL YOU"

"When he said those words, my heart almost stopped." Christine placed the palm of her hand over the center of her chest for emphasis. During the past two years, there had been a series of signs that Jay, the man with whom she was obsessively in love, was not of a mind to reciprocate. Up until now, however, he had managed to shift the responsibility for his inability to make a commitment to a lack of confidence in himself and in his future, rather than to a deficiency of deep feelings for Christine. It was what she had wanted to hear and was therefore only too willing to accept.

What made the present state of this relationship so different, and so unbearable, was that, for reasons unknown to her, Jay had decided to abandon his former tactics of diplomatic evasiveness. At least, for this occasion he would be honest to a fault, and honesty required that he tell her that his feelings for her "had changed," that whatever love he had or thought he had for her in the past was no longer there and was not likely to return. Nor could he explain why this had happened. He had not wanted it to happen. So far as he could tell, he had done nothing to make it happen. It had in fact happened to him. All he was certain of was that he no longer had any interest in pursuing the relationship in a serious manner.

A side effect of the profound impairment of the capacity to be intimate that is characteristic of our time is that one increasingly feels the need to bail out of involvements that are perceived as stressful. More and more, relationships are appraised not in terms of how value-laden or meaningful they are but according to the tension they engender. When that tension passes a subjectively determined critical threshold, the person may feel the need for quick relief, as well as a reassurance that the intolerable situation is not to be repeated. Should the tension be perceived as emanating from another individual in whom one is invested, the person, in the manner of Christine's boyfriend, may elect to cut himself free, swiftly and once and for all, from the burdensome baggage of the now unwanted relationship. Such relational surgery is often euphemistically called honest confrontation. Confrontational, yes—but is it honest?

Typically, a confrontation between two people is regarded as a kind of weeding-out of noxious psychic elements in an interpersonal situation that is viewed by at least one person as heading in the direction of a crisis. In the service of saving valuable time, the assumption is made that everything should be eliminated except the bare bones of the points of contention. A confrontation is therefore an insistence on addressing what is deemed to be the heart of the problem. There is a tone of urgency as though the crucial period in which to deal with the issue has finally arrived and, unless acted upon, might be irretrievably lost. A confrontational stance therefore implies that the one who is confronting is more prepared and more aware of what needs to be done than the one who is being confronted and to that extent is like an interpersonal alarm.

To the other, a confrontation is almost never welcome because it represents the extreme of someone interacting from the vantage point of a psychical running head start (akin to the person who complains or is stubborn) and cannot help but elicit resentful feelings of being driven involuntarily into a competitive arena.

Yet to be confrontational, while appearing dramatic and interactive, is often no more than to be pseudo-dialogic. On the one hand, it suggests that the person has a burning desire to engage the other, perhaps more earnestly than he ever has; on the other hand, there is the message that the confronter has passed well beyond the stage of dialogue and intersubjective communication and (probably in solitude) has arrived at the conviction that action is what is needed.

The one who is being confronted, therefore, can feel doubly pressured: to agree first with the assessment that the time for idle conversing or playing around is over and second that a change in the relationship (as proposed by the confronter) is not only appropriate but long overdue. From the standpoint of the other, this is a demand that cannot autonomously be met. Accordingly, he will suspect that what he is really being asked to do is to *comply*, and not surprisingly his initial impulse will be to try to dodge the impending confrontation if at all possible. Such resistance, however, is often anticipated and countered with an attempt to nip it in the bud by bringing even more pressure to bear.

What usually ensues are tactics designed to bully the other who is perceived as unlikely to do what is deemed necessary unless coerced into doing so. From a psychodynamic perspective, therefore, a confrontation is really an effort to hem a person in, cut off his probable avenues of escape, grab him by the conversational lapels, and force a showdown. It does this by unexpectedly interjecting a dramatically heightened level of gravity to the relationship that characteristically surpasses anything that preceded it.

Thus, a classic segue to an intended confrontation is: "I have something I'd like to talk to you about." The effect of this— analogous to that of the individual who responds with surprising stubbornness to what was perceived by the other as thoroughly unremarkable—is generally to grind the ongoing interaction to a painful stop, but the difference is that there is a suggestion of a future. Something has to be done now, so that a situation that has become unbearable can change sometime soon. There is perhaps a sense of an ultimatum or, at the very least, that a turning point has been reached. But it is a turning point that only the confronter seems to realize and it is this powerful message to the other, that he is being pressed to participate in a possible showdown, that rivets his attention and makes it almost impossible to entertain any other course of action except to address the matter of contention.

The one who is being approached in such a fashion is therefore neatly hemmed in: if he ignores the confrontation, he runs the risk of escalating it. (The non-argumentative but unmistakable tone of high moral ground which usually accompanies a confrontational stance makes avoidance exceedingly awkward.)

What he can do (and often does) is to offer some token effort to consider the issue being raised, in the hope of defusing the latent tension that invariably is present, while simultaneously conspiring to get away as soon as possible so he can attempt to figure out how this terrible impasse has arisen.

Here, in schematized form, is a bare-bones scenario of a typical confrontation, one that is heard frequently in the office of a therapist (C stands for the confronter and O for the other):

C: There is something I've been wanting to say to you
     for awhile.
O: You want to talk to me about something?
C: Yes.
O: Okay.
C: For a long time I've felt that whenever I'm with
     you and say anything to you, you seem to take it for
     granted. I don't feel you really listen to me, and when-
     ever you do respond, it seems like you're really bored.
O: That's not my experience. I'm sorry you feel that way.
C: Well, I do.
O: Let me tell you that I *do* take you seriously. But
     thank you for making me aware of your feelings.
C: I just wanted you to know how I felt.

It is indeed rare when a confrontation achieves what it presumably sets out to do—effect a meaningful change in a situation that is perceived as unacceptable if not unbearable, and this example is no exception. Instead of real contact, or even a semblance of honest communication about a sensitive issue, there is a kind of stiff-legged, ceremonious power struggle. As the example shows, the one who initiates the confrontation characteristically harbors little expectation of being empathized with and even less, as mentioned, of being autonomously given to. It is therefore understandable that it will take almost all of his courage just to state in simple language the gist of his grievance: in this instance, that he feels not only taken for granted but consistently written off as someone uninteresting and boring.

Accordingly, he does not really believe that the other is likely to voluntarily change her mind upon being informed of his narcissistic injury. Instead he correctly anticipates that at best he will be offered polite and face-saving denial (e. g., "That's not my experience"). This in turn will evoke a milder, second-tier confrontation, meant to deliver the message that he intends to stand by his guns ("Well, I do").

Anyone who has felt driven to gather his courage by revealing the highly unpleasant, intensely embarrassing fact that he is aware that the other views him as essentially a bore will appreciate how great the temptation is to believe, against all evidence, that only a mistake has been made and to therefore accept the typically disingenuous apology that is proffered ("I'm sorry you feel that way"). By flatly resisting such a temptation, the person reaffirms his position and thereby continues the confrontational stance. But only for a moment. Upon receiving a second denial ("Let me tell you that I do take you seriously . . . ") the person, in effect, capitulates ("Okay").

In the great majority of confrontational interpersonal enactments, little more than this occurs. Someone screws up his courage to communicate a stored-up, simmering feeling that certain behavior on the part of another has become patently offensive. The other, alarmed at the unexpected gravity of a situation that was presumed to be under control, nervously tries to defuse the potential threat with a mixture of denial, apology, and pretended deference. Sensing that at most he is only being placated, the confronter endeavors to put teeth into his assertion by reasserting it, to which the other answers with stepped-up protestations of unimpeachable good faith. It is at this juncture that the person is faced with the difficult decision of whether to honestly challenge the pseudo-relating that is being used to deny the considerable tension that hangs in the air (and thereby run the risk of increasing it) or, by grasping at the spurious closure that is routinely offered, to back down instead.

Because it is not only painful but generally unrewarding to initiate confrontation, most people elect to quickly back down. One of two things then happens. The initiator, pleased with the determination displayed by his bold disclosure and partially gratified by the other's show of deference, rewards himself by retreating to the safety of the old (if aggravating) relationship. Or, in a contrary scenario, his original impression of being taken for granted, reinforced by his sense that the other is only pretending to take his present complaint seriously (once again taking him for granted), he can conclude that it would be pointless to continue to swallow his resentment. He can then write off the relationship and justify his withdrawal by reminding himself that the cat is out of the bag anyway: he has made it crystal clear that he intensely disapproves of what has been going on interpersonally between himself and the other.

From the standpoint of intimacy, it is obvious that nothing substantive occurs in this type of interaction. This follows from the fact that the one who initiates the confrontation characteristically does not expect to be understood, empathized with, or given to in any meaningful way. Although he often hopes for the satisfaction of getting something important off his chest, he also fears that his disclosure may trigger retaliation. He therefore attempts to nip this imagined counterattack in the bud by channeling his available psychic energies into a preemptive strike meant to impose a premature closure.

Since the person who chooses to take the first confrontational step cannot help but remember the period of bottled-up resentment and sense of suppression that often precedes it, he is hardly likely to enter the fray with an air of true confidence. Instead, he will probably adopt the psychological version of a hit-and-run tactic: by suddenly disclosing the bare bones of his biggest gripe, he will have gotten in at least one good punch in the ensuing conflict. That's the hit part. The run part—given that the prospect of seriously challenging someone who so far has succeeded (wittingly or unwittingly) in intimidating him into keeping silent must be somewhat scary—is the almost irresistible temptation to collude by accepting the pseudo-resolution that is usually proffered.

It is instructive to compare this very ordinary kind of confrontation with what therapists sometimes describe as a "good" confrontation, a transaction that is in the service of improved mental health—in this case, a disclosure that is deemed necessary to achieve a richer, deeper level of engagement with a particular person with whom one is involved. While every therapist will have his or her distinctive criteria for appraising the therapeutic potential of a specific encounter, here are mine:

First of all, for an aggressive engagement of the other to have at least a chance of moving in the direction of intimacy, it cannot in any way be coercive in the sense I have been depicting. Instead, it must be *facilitating*. By facilitating, I mean it will begin by clearing the way for mutuality, spontaneity, and autonomous interaction by recognizing the right of the other to initially and flatly decline to join in a confrontational encounter. If, however, the other does express a willingness to participate in an unusually candid discussion about whatever seems to be bothering the person about the relationship, there will be an awareness of the degree of anxiety that the raising of the issue may be evoking in the other. In short, the person who feels compelled to elevate the tension level of the preexisting relationship will realize that the needs of the one who is being confronted, while perhaps less urgent, are no less important. Although this may seem obvious, it is striking how often the confronter's sense of entitlement when it comes to righting a wrong that has been suffered in silence simply obliterates any balanced perception of the other's point of view (which may, of course, be substantially different).

Thus, to be confrontational and empathic at the same time is a considerable feat. It happens rarely because, in part, the intention to be confrontational, especially for the first time, generally arouses strong anticipatory anxiety as the person struggles to find the best way to break the ice. The situation is not unlike that of trying to figure out how to ask someone out on a date, or how to make an initial move towards physical intimacy, or how to tell someone you are involved with you no longer wish to see them. Understandably, the person would like to handle the situation as he has tried to handle most situations in his life: in small, safe, manageable, and, if possible, comfortable steps.

However, since the situations we are describing all have in common that they entail taking a step that is experienced as a substantial risk (that of incurring devastating rejection) there is no such thing as a safe, comfortable way to do it. It is the combination of these two factors—the anxious uncertainty over pursuing a course of action deemed necessary but fraught with danger and the inability to reassure oneself that nothing terrible will happen—that results in the familiar, panicky attempt to overcontrol, orchestrate, and force to a premature closure a transaction that in actuality requires significant tact and empathy, as well as patient resolve, to carry off.

But such is out of the question for our nervous confronter. Typically, he will begin in the manner of someone who is about to jump off a particularly high diving board for the first time: he will try to still his beating heart and, in a moment of keen anxiety, push himself across a point of no return. The radical discontinuity that is often felt at these times, the unnerving sense that one is on the brink of moving dangerously out on a limb, derives from the realization that there is no simple safe passage from the penultimate moment—just before one jumps from the diving board or, in our example, announces to the other he has something of great import to iron out concerning the relationship—to the moment of truth. It follows that the most one can hope for in such adverse circumstances is survival, that is, to concentrate almost all of one's available energies on what appears to be most threatening.

If someone, therefore, has made a decision to broach a major sore point in a relationship with another person for the first time, the very real possibility of the other's stubborn resistance, anger, or retaliation is what most threatens. The thrust of the transaction will most likely be to deliver one's main points as effectively and (hopefully) as briefly as one can, while trying to contain the defensive interference of the other, which typically is viewed negatively as an angry attempt to prolong the confrontational tension.

However, since it is nearly impossible to control the response of the other without some kind of glitch, there is usually resistance—characteristically in the form of assertive denial and compliant apology, which are often collusively joined to produce a dishonest amnesty.

From an interpersonal standpoint, a confrontation is a transaction that poses as the quintessence of fearless disclosure and candid, heart-to-heart conversation, but in reality is often the antithesis of true intimacy.

LIKE IT IS

Twenty years ago, while still a graduate student, I participated in a gestalt therapy workshop led by Dr. Rudolph Roland, a well-known and enthusiastic proponent of the technique known as the "hot seat." As pioneered by the legendary Fritz Perls, one of the godfathers of the encounter movement that reached its pinnacle in the '70s, this was meant to be a necessarily painful but ultimately benign procedure wherein a person's maladaptive defenses are mercilessly peeled away. All that is required is for a subject to voluntarily occupy the empty, ordinary-looking chair standing at the head of the room designated as the "hot seat" and to allow the manner in which he expresses himself, in particular his non-verbal behavior, to be publicly scrutinized by the leader.

Not surprisingly, only two of the eight who attended the workshop were bold enough to sit in the hot seat and both seemed to regret it almost immediately. Dr. Roland, a huge, utterly self-assured man, had situated himself in a sideways position to his subjects and for the most part he seemed intent to ponder in deep thought their squirming profiles. When he did speak, he did not mince words and as one listened to him, it became clear after a while that nothing seemed to please him.

The two volunteers had been, in his view, anything but truly open: alternately assuming a role, going through the motions, being exhibitionistic, wasting the class's time and especially his, playing games, or perhaps downright lying. In fact, during the hour and a half that the two guinea pigs occupied the hot seat, he could not recollect a single instance of honest self-expression. It was an observation that only bolstered his belief that in this country people find it extraordinarily difficult to be direct.

As though to prove his point that people shun being direct because it stirs up anxiety, Dr. Roland seemed to go out of his way to say exactly what was on his mind. When a student inquired, for example, in regard to a description by Dr. Roland of his work with a suicidally depressed woman, whether it was boring to be with a near catatonic patient, he replied, "Well, she was more alive than you," and when I, beguiled by psychoanalytic theory at that time, wondered aloud if part of the expanded awareness that is the goal of the gestalt technique included manifestations of the unconscious, Dr. Roland instantly retorted, "If you're aware of it, it is not unconscious." Feeling more dismissed than answered, I decided to ask for clarification—an action that drew the observation, "I think I'm beginning to pick up that you're a pest."

Twenty years later, Dr. Roland's encounter jargon and admonition to "be direct" have been translated into the popular motto, "Tell it like it is." The underlying concept, however, does not appear to have changed. To be *direct*, it should be noted, does not mean the same as to be *confrontive* (as in the previous example), although being confrontive is supposed to be based on being direct. The difference between being direct and being confrontive might be that between honestly facing your feelings as opposed to honestly addressing a conflict between yourself and another person. This means that, from the standpoint of interpersonal communication, the distance between point A (what the person basically feels) and point B (the clarity and brevity with which he expresses it) is presumably the shortest possible one. It follows that, for this to be the case, there has to be (if not an absence) a minimum of defensive filtering. And, accordingly, there is the assumption whenever in the presence of someone who is strikingly direct that the defensive need to edit what the person really thinks and feels has been sufficiently worked through so that a thorough and uncontaminated disclosure can be made.

Seen that way, the individual who is direct will be unbiased by superego prohibitions or psychic censoring. Such a person will say what is on his mind and in his heart almost as though reading without a hitch from an inner cue card with a minimum of processing. In reality, of course, this is impossible, and what is taken for being direct (as is particularly clear in the example of Dr. Roland) is often instances of someone being only rude or crude. (The rationale for such behavior, as in the use of the pseudo-real, is that only the force of the real could break through the various social inhibitions that guard against someone creating unnecessary anxiety by coming too quickly to the point, especially when the other is not prepared for it.)

The conventional folk wisdom that guards against someone being direct in this manner can therefore be seen as a recognition of the necessity of buying time to allow one or both parties to stumble on an unpleasant social or interpersonal truth (if there is one to be found) at their own, more congenial pace. This can be more readily understood if it is remembered just how uncomfortable it is to be around someone known for their unfailing candor, that is, someone who at any moment is capable of telling you he either strongly disapproves of what you have just said or done, is becoming bored in your presence, or does not respect you as a person.

Compounding the problem is that those who are committed to "telling it like it is" characteristically do not seem to realize that there are few who are willing to risk being in their presence. That is because other people intuitively sense that only someone with a remarkable paucity of empathy can insist on venting without censorship whatever comes into mind on almost any issue. For that reason, someone with a reputation for uncompromising frankness often turns out to be essentially relating only to his own narcissistic need to be as unfettered as possible in whatever he chooses to express. Since, however, in genuine dialogue the needs of the auditor are as important as the needs of the speaker, such a person is really delivering the message that there is just one voice that matters. It follows that people who are viewed as exceedingly direct are usually considered to be non-reciprocally so: they are found to be predictably emphatic when it comes to being a spokesman for their own myriad subjective states of mind, but *not* when it comes to being a non-biased receiver for the communicational input of the other.

It is therefore hardly surprising that people who are notorious for their outspokenness tend to be admired from afar, like talk show celebrities or anti-establishment sports heroes, but are feared up close. There are reasons for this. As already mentioned, someone seen as direct (analogous to the person who relates in a confrontational, complaining, or stubborn fashion) is regarded as having a considerable head start from the vantage point of available emotional energy (with the unfortunate result that the other almost automatically tends to think in terms of defending rather than expressing himself). In order to have arrived at such a strongly felt and centered opinion (enviable for its perceived lack of ambiguity), such a person is presumed to have worked through a number of intrapsychic and interpersonal impediments. Now it is thought he can express himself unequivocally about what he thinks and feels because he *is* unequivocal about what he thinks and feels (as opposed to expressing himself unequivocably because he is impulsive and cannot tolerate uncertainty, anxiety, and suspense but instead craves the grandiose reassurance that comes from immediate discharge).

For all these reasons, a typical response to a surprisingly direct self-disclosure is to become introverted and even immobilized. One senses one is not likely to match the level of forthrightness displayed, and that anything less would disqualify one from being taken seriously. In most instances, therefore, someone who is direct tends to inhibit the other from responding in kind, or, to put it more directly, *being direct elicits indirectness from the other.*

Not for long, though. When the resentment stemming from feeling suppressed builds sufficiently, it can erupt in retaliatory attempts not only to compete with but even, on occasion, to outshine the other in forthrightness. (Once again, akin to expressive actions that are perceived as complaining or confrontive, it tends to command the modeling of behavior that in almost any other context would be perceived as negative.)

From the perspective of interpersonal relations, someone who comes across as unambiguously straightforward will also appear to have arrived at closure. Since "telling it like it is" seems to imply an absence of an unconscious (with, therefore, no need for defenses), it suggests there is scant possibility that another point of view will add anything new or useful. Accordingly, it is typically presented as a conversational fait accompli, something verbally as plain as the nose on your face. Being direct seems to imply that whatever needs to be said has just been said and, perhaps more significantly, that what has not been said does not *need* to be said. It is as though a definitive statement of thought and feeling has been rendered and closure has therefore beyond doubt been reached. The person says, in effect, "I have nothing more to say on this topic." In itself this is intimidating and quite controlling because the implicit assumptions are: (1) there is nothing relevant that you can add, and (2) there is nothing that you may think is relevant that you would like to add that I would want to hear. All of this contributes to a second-level message: the subject is closed.

This will sound familiar, from our previous discussion of confrontation, as another example of premature closure coercively imposed on the other. The difference, however, is that in a transaction that can be characterized as confrontive, closure is projected into a dialogue supposed to take place in the immediate future, while the case of someone being direct is more like issuing a proclamation in the present of a personal matter that has already been privately settled. What they both share, however, is that they kill off any movement toward intersubjectivity: the confrontation by its forcing manner, and the unmediated direct assertion by its aura of broadcasting unvarnished information about the self—the antithesis of an authentic invitation to playful dialogue.

ROLE PLAYING

Seemingly a role can release a person from the responsibility of being a whole human being. It can be perceived as social permission to become (at least for the duration of the role) not an existential person, but a functional one. To that extent, it can be taken as an injunction to engage in a willing suspension of existential needs. What is forgotten is that this is all but impossible: no matter how pressing the functional or performance requirements are, there is always a need for a certain validation of the true self that cannot with impunity be brushed aside.

Someone who seriously immerses himself in the playing out of a traditional role (in particular a professional or business one) can engender immediate suspicion and even resentment in the onlooker that the role player is perhaps only hiding behind his performance and that therefore the other is being existentially cheated. This suspiciousness is most in abeyance when the person feels that his needs are being well served by the functional aspects of the role. Even then, however, there is often curiosity about the parts of the self that conceivably could be buried beneath the manifest behavioral components of the transaction. Such curiosity typically fastens on the question, "Would he be so nice to me if he didn't have to be, and what does he actually think of me?"

By contrast, it follows that such suspiciousness will most likely come to the fore when the needs of the other are not being met or when it may become necessary either to bend the rules or make an outright exception to them. It is clear that the role player then has to make a choice: stick to the literal conduct code of the role or deviate by venturing to make an autonomous creative application. The dilemma for the individual who wishes to conscientiously carry out his role is that the prescribed code of conduct cannot by its nature provide for creative surprises, nor can it be expected to cope with the request for the presence of the true self. All it can offer on such occasions is the palliative of mechanical relating (a forced air of cheerful tranquillity), special training in how to deal with dissatisfied customers, and what I call the *technique of intimacy*. This is another way of saying that the specific dynamics arising from this existential need for affirmation cannot, by definition, be treated as information or as something that can be taught. On some level the other knows this and will wait to see if the person is going to retreat into the safety of role compliance or, instead, in a move toward role transcendence, make some kind of authentic self-statement. And it is because the other has learned from personal experience that such role transcendence in the service of the self is becoming exceedingly rare (especially in our increasingly overspecialized, high-tech society) that he often tends to overreact with immediate and sometimes aggressive mistrust.

It follows that there will be resistance not only (classically) to the role of the psychotherapist, but to any role that subordinates the true self of the person to the operational exigencies, either business or professional, of the here and now. In practice this means that there is an attempt to drive the person out of the role and a substantial part of role playing, therefore, will be to maintain the integrity of the role in the face of such predictable interpersonal pressure to desert it. Maintaining the integrity of a role frequently comes down to going out of one's way to accentuate the impersonal features of the particular role.

All of which is nicely illustrated by the following incident, recounted to me by a patient (a woman to be referred to as the customer) as she complains bitterly about her treatment by a male cashier, who, it appeared to her, was unnecessarily and even oppressively strict.

Cashier: I'm sorry. It's five o'clock. The register's closed.

Customer: But I've been waiting in line for nearly forty-five minutes.

Cashier: They announced over twenty minutes ago that the store would be closing in five minutes.

Customer: It'll be at least two full weeks before I can get back down here again.

Cashier: There's nothing I can do. That's the policy.

Note that the more resentful and frustrated the customer becomes, the more she strives to break through the armor of the role to the interior self of the cashier: she tries harder to appeal to a person and not to a company policy ("But I've been waiting in line for nearly forty-five minutes"). In turn, the cashier, refusing to relinquish his role as guardian of the company's rule, reinforces it by mildly lecturing the customer on her negligent behavior ("They announced twenty minutes ago that the store would be closing in five minutes").

Thus the more one aims to induce the other to personalize the relationship, the more the other retaliates by responding in an impersonal manner. And the more tension there is between them, the more this is so: the more the one asks for or insists upon empathy, the more the other retreats into mean-spirited officiousness.

How tenaciously someone clings to a role therefore becomes evident whenever the other attempts to relate to him in a non-role-playing manner. There are reasons for this. A role seems to release a person from the requirement to be a whole human being. Furthermore, it offers tempting access to a ready-made functional identity—one that can be specified and then quantified along a graduated continuum of measurable levels of stipulated performance. A comparison of a functional identity with a psychical one founded on a self that cannot ever be quantified shows why there can be comfort in the arbitrary parameters that are an intrinsic part of any designated role and why it can seem as though one is being granted an identity as opposed to having to discover or actualize a cohesive sense of self. From such a perspective, it can appear that one has been liberated from the universal burden of having to choose and to decide, and instead has only to follow instructions and to execute. To that extent, playing a role can seem as though one has been given permission to behave in a relatively nonautonomous fashion, or, rather, to be autonomous only to the degree that one is free to determine how and when to do what one feels one *has* to do.

From the viewpoint of the other it is often frustrating (as in the example given) to be related to by someone adhering to a strict code of conduct, especially when it is believed that the best way one's real needs can be met is by having the person either step outside of the role he is assuming or put much more of his true self into what he is doing. Such hopes tend to be disappointed, however, because the person—in order to compensate for the existential impoverishment that follows from having to perform according to a rigid code of behavior—is often driven to overidentify with the power of the role.

What is overlooked is that a role can be used as a negation of direct intimate contact between two people. The very implication that functional performance aims are superordinate to relational ones is itself trivializing. This is because the existential need to have one's presence affirmed as making a meaningful difference is ongoing and by its nature cannot simply be relegated to the back burner.

Optimally, a role should be in the service of the true self of the person and its continuation should be predicated on how well it discharges that service. When it fails to do that, the person has the option of stepping outside the role or of expanding its parameters by investing himself more fully in it. It would have been easy for this to have transpired in the example given: the cashier would have had only to make a single exception to the company rule that the register must be closed by five o'clock or, if that was not possible, to have at least genuinely empathized with the considerable inconvenience, not to speak of narcissistic injury, that the customer would have to suffer by being refused service after standing in line for nearly forty-five minutes.

It is obvious that roles are rarely enacted in the optimal fashion I have just described. Far more often are they used as hiding places. In the sense that a role can legitimize functional needs over existential ones, it can, as shown, seemingly offer a reprieve from the pressure to be authentic, to act from a personal center, and to be ever cognizant of the uniqueness of one's identity. From this relational standpoint, someone who assumes a role buys time. Due to its peculiar yet characteristic ambivalence, it is in practice extremely difficult, short of a conflict, to tell whether an individual role player has subordinated the given role to the needs of the true self or, contrariwise, has at least temporarily sacrificed his core identity on the altar of opportunism and operationalism.

Normally, ambivalence betrays itself in an interpersonal setting through its alternation of dissonant modalities of behavior. However, by incorporating such psychic ambivalence into its basic structure, a role can seem to promise a seductive escape from the abiding interpersonal need to integrate self and other into some kind of meaningful interaction. It does this by conferring meaning on the basis of performance and approval rating, while simultaneously discounting the value of relationship. In so doing, it unconsciously and automatically degrades the necessity for existential affirmation. If performance (and not the true self) is what is to be validated, it then becomes easy to rationalize the abandonment of genuine intimacy needs in favor of the implementation of role aims. What is more, according to this insidious way of thinking (pervasive in our culture) one is then not only not avoiding one's responsibility to be more humanly intimate by acting in a perfunctory, rule-bound manner, but one is admirably enhancing one's proficiency.

What is not appreciated is the degree of control thereby available to the person who cannot otherwise justify being non-intimate and who, abetted by the premium our increasingly technological and compartmentalized society places on role playing, can now say either that instead of being non-intimate he is simply carrying out the requirements of the role (as, for example, the person who explains, "If I don't work late almost every night, I'll lose my job") or conversely, that he is being non-intimate because, in this case, intimacy is not called for and would in fact interfere with something substantially more important—the discharge of responsibility.

It is worth noting that in this type of defense, relationship and intimacy are often treated somewhat scornfully as luxuries that cannot be afforded. It is another matter, however, when the sense of role responsibility is not to a job (where culturally it is reinforced) but to the performance of familial duties such as being a good provider, caretaker, or parental educator and disciplinarian to one's children. When that is the case and the ideas of personal familial responsibility and nurturant intimacy are somehow compartmentalized, people can arrive at the following paradoxical belief: that it is possible to be conscientiously parental and familial without having to be simultaneously kind, empathic, and attuned to the innermost selves of those to whom one is supposedly relating in a loving manner (often expressed in the classic rationalizations "You'll thank me for this one day" or "I'm doing this for you").

This is more easily understood when it is considered how hard it is for two consenting adults to invest in one another in a serious, nurturing, and committed way. One reason it is so difficult is that in our contemporary culture, unless two people have been living together for a substantial period of time, there is almost absolute freedom to break the bond at any moment, whenever one feels like it. What this means is that the temptation to avoid the engulfment threats of protracted intimacy by escaping from the relationship can prove for many people an offer that cannot be refused. At the other end of the continuum are spousal and parental affiliations where there are at least prescribed financial and legal penalties to pay for impulsive acts of desertion. It is worth noting that the common denominator between these two polarities of commitment, from the standpoint of intimacy, is still an autonomous investment of the true self, an attunement to and a profound nurturance of the primary needs of the other.

Now, while admittedly the achievement of the state of intimacy is no mean feat for two consenting adults to pull off in the face of the omnipresent freedom to abandon the relationship, it is that much more difficult to accomplish when someone is constantly under the gun to honor the fundamental obligations of a traditional familial role (spousal or parental). Since a traditional role customarily carries with it emphatic behavioral, operational, and performance expectations—things that *must* be done—a person's conception of how to manageably discharge such a full-time responsibility will almost invariably be contaminated by feelings of effort, burden, and sometimes coercion. And when there are feelings of being coerced, it is extremely likely they will be represented, sometimes overtly, in the enactment of the role.

Because of such pressure, there is often a manifest undercurrent of resentment in even the best and bravest of mothers, fathers, husbands, and wives. It is, accordingly, not a simple matter for even the agent himself to tell whether he is doing what he is doing because he wants to or has to. It is even more difficult for the beneficiary to tell. When the beneficiary is a child, it is practically impossible to tell. This is compounded by the parents' perception of children as generally harmless, which means they are freer to be self-indulgent and irresponsible without caring about the consequences of their behavior. A principal way for people to be irresponsible in their roles as parents is to believe that they can separate out the performance need from the need for intimacy.

In practice, this comes down to the almost universal habit of first getting children to do what they are supposed to do (homework, eating their meals, brushing their teeth, going to bed, and so on) and then showing—when there is protest or crying at an act of discipline perceived as unfair—reparative empathy. However, nurturance and empathy with the child's feelings are most useful *during* the role enactment (when the parent is actually engaged in educative or disciplinary actions) because that is when the child experiences the most tension and greatest need for support. It is also the time when the child is most likely to feel misunderstood or abandoned in no small part because he can sense that the parent is basically relating to his or her own need to be temporarily rid of the pressure, the guilt, and the burden associated with his proper management. In turn, the child will resent his parents' resentment of the role they seem to be stuck with, because he will (correctly) sense the self-involvement which underlies it.

It is at this juncture that the great cop-out, "I'm only doing this for your own good," will probably be pressed into service. Seen this way, a role offers, not only to parents but to almost everyone, a kind of fail-safe shield behind which a person can hide whatever issues he has with intimacy. If one is in the mood, one can place the role in the service of empathy and strive for attunement with the other's needs. If one is unable to be intimate, one can simply assert that the demands of the role do not allow it and that there are more important things at hand than the wish for intimacy. Thus, donning a role can, among other things, offer the illusion of having access to a secret psychic light switch enabling one at will to turn on or off one's needs for intimacy without anyone being the wiser and thereby seemingly gaining control over something that cannot really be controlled—the flow of spontaneous, authentic human interactivity.

BEING NEEDY

A patient, Rachel, is complaining about a neighbor, a man she originally considered to be quite friendly in a harmless sort of way, but about whom she has begun to have second thoughts.

When I met him in the laundromat of my building for the first time, I thought he was nice. He talked on and on about everything he and his fiancée thought was wrong about the building and since I had just moved in and am suspicious by nature, I thought I'd found an ally.

But I changed my mind the very next time I saw him. I was in the elevator, the door opened, and there he was. He seemed so happy to see me that I thought it was ridiculous. Without even waiting to see what my reaction or mood was, he began talking about some New Year's Eve party he was looking forward to and how he had therefore elected his fiancée to be his designated driver. I wasn't at all interested, but that didn't seem to deter him. He just kept jabbering away. When we got to street level, I pretended to be going in a direction opposite to his just to get away from him.

Now, I do everything I can to avoid him. If I'm about to step into a crowded elevator on the lobby floor and see out of the corner of my eye that he's standing in the rear of the car, I pull back and wait for the next elevator. If I'm walking outside and see him first, I try to duck out of sight. Once in a

while, of course, the elevator door opens and there he is. He
continues to corner me and talk only about himself, but he's
aware I'm barely responding to him, which makes him all the
more desperate to capture my attention.

Rachel, of course, is exquisitely sensitive to people who
attempt to use her for their own ends, and this recent neighbor is just one in a series of men and women who have irri-
tated her with their self-involvement. When I asked her just
what she objected to so much in this man, she replied without
missing a beat, "his neediness," and then proceeded to describe
his (to her) prominent emotion-filled brown eyes, which she
despised.

Although not everyone is as acutely aware of its impact as
Rachel, neediness as a state of being is rather common. It is
often viewed as the psychical antithesis of maturity or the role
responsibility described in the previous section. Someone
is regarded as needy when their wants become so intrusive
they cannot be ignored by self or other. This is because people
generally try either to deny inappropriate needs or to express
them in the form of ulterior motives or hidden agendas. Since
excessive vulnerability is regarded in our culture as a clear sign
of weakness, of not being in control, the fact that someone is
visibly unable to disguise his neediness seems proof of just how
dominant his impulses are.

Such a person can appear self-involved to a threatening
degree. Typically, social transactions are conceived as a dynamic
bartering between self and other where it is understood that
there will never be a parity of need satisfaction but where there
is at least the hope of obtaining an occasionally meaningful if
partial gratification. In the case of the aggressively needy person, however, it is obvious there can be little prospect of sharing in the benefits of mutuality and that one cannot realisti-

cally hope to be nurtured by someone who is overtly laboring to ward off feelings of engulfing deprivation.

Moreover, there is the sense that unless one is especially alert, one can at any moment be swept up into the service of the person's neediness. Such a person automatically engenders resentment because the other feels it necessary either to constantly say no or to be ready to say no in order not to be considerably more compliant than one would normally like to be. It is natural to anxiously and resentfully wonder what this person will want and when he is going to ask for it. Accordingly, he is viewed as not only impulsive but shamefully so, inasmuch as there does not seem to be any evidence of an attempt to contain the drive for satisfaction. On the contrary, he acts as though entitled to blatantly feed his ravenousness and it is this perception of the uninhibited pursuit of gratification that makes him seem not merely needy, but greedy as well. The perception of need powered by greed tends to be self-cancelling and the other, not surprisingly, feels justified not to respond to someone who increasingly is regarded as a psychological beggar. It is no simple matter, however, not to respond in view of the fact that the other feels that the pressure is always more or less on to give more than she wants to give. (One popular strategy is to relate with exaggerated, courteous attentiveness as if to reassure the person that the inner decision not to give is based neither on indifference nor the inability to really hear what someone is saying.)

Thus, to experience someone as intrusively needy is to almost irresistibly be driven into a restricted interpersonal field of strategic relating that, by definition, cannot allow for directness. How many times in your life have you heard one person say to another, "I think you are being too needy?" It is the type of thing, except in the hands of an expert at "hot seat" confrontation, that rarely gets said in our society. Such an individual, reinforced by the conspiracy of silence, is thereby encouraged to continue his solicitations.

Sensing there is no easy way of either satisfying or discouraging someone who seems swamped by his wants, the other usually settles for an intermediate course of cordial avoidance. Her basic interpersonal aim is to escape the needy person. And even if she entertained the diametrically opposite aim, to fully gratify his voracious emotional appetite, it would be exceedingly difficult to do so because of its undifferentiated nature. By contrast, it is of the essence of a well-defined aim that it is specific. Being specific implies choice, and choosing entails, among other things, a consideration of what to eliminate and what to hold on to, which in turn requires restraint. But, since the needy individual is aware that he lacks the discipline to restrict himself to the gratification of one appropriate aim at a time, he tries to cover himself by not leaving anything out. Most commonly this is done by communicating a general state of need instead of specifying what is wanted. What this individual is really asking for, then, is not one reasonable thing but the recognition that he is in a condition of deprivation that requires the full attention of the other. It is as if he is saying, "I'm not sure what I need, other than that I do need a lot, and it's important for you to realize this and put on hold whatever you're doing and stand on call for me."

No one, of course (and certainly not the typical chronically insecure, needy person), can admit this and so we have the familiar attitude of pushy charm—a reparative sop for the discomfort being imposed upon the other, who in effect is being asked to relate not to a person but to a state of impoverishment. The other, realizing the hollow seductiveness of such impulse-driven sociability, will often try to defuse the disavowed pressure tactics with diversionary pleasantries. This is another way of saying that the individual who is overtly, aggressively needy almost irresistibly lures the other into a modeling kind of manipulative interrelating that forecloses any chance of incipient intimacy.

"I'M SORRY"

Many years ago while working as an intern in an alcoholism rehabilitation center, I encountered my first professional psychologist; Bonnie, a precocious young woman, at the tender age of 26 was in the process of completing her doctoral thesis in clinical psychology. Not at all shy about her newly acquired expertise, she was fond of spouting interpretations (so-called psychodynamically based insights into the unconscious motivation of people in everyday actions) whenever someone said or did something that seemed to her provocatively ambivalent. Thus, when one of the unit's secretaries came up to her and profusely apologized for apparently having temporarily mislaid one of her psychological reports, Bonnie instantly analyzed the interaction. "Don't say you're sorry. That's asking unconscious permission to repeat the behavior."

Obviously, it was a remark that made an impact on me, because years later, as I am trying to think of an example that shows the tremendous controlling power of the words "I'm sorry," I can still recall it. What Bonnie had put her finger on, in her bold, confrontational manner, was the ulterior motive of the apologist to defuse the potential aggressive intentions of the other. So effective in our culture is the brief, spontaneous apology that it can seem to be almost the linguistic equivalent of an ethological fixed-action pattern of appeasement.

Although the efficiency of an apology may seem obvious, the dynamics are far from simple. Typically, the apologist communicates by a combination of word and gesture that he is in an immediate state of genuine penitence for the unwitting harm that may have been committed to an innocent other. It is clear that expressing aggression toward such a person would be tantamount to attacking a mourner. At the same time, however, professing to be sorry is admitting there is something to be sorry for—usually an action or recent behavior of the person for which he is customarily held responsible, as opposed, for example, to simply being the auditor of the other's misfortune (such as a death in the family). What "I'm sorry" is meant to accomplish, is to transform what may have been experienced as a thoughtless or aggressive act—bumping into him, damaging a piece of his property, or in some way encroaching on his territory—into a purely accidental one. Someone who proclaims he is sorry in effect completely disavows agency and responsibility for what he allegedly has done.

But he does more than dissociate himself from any intent to harm. He strives to make instant reparation by proclaiming his state of mourning, dramatizing that he is not only not callously or aggressively indifferent to the pain he has caused but is empathic enough to become at once contrite for any harm unwittingly rendered. By thereby diverting the other's attention to a display of his own distress, he hopes to nip in the bud any potential eruption of retaliative anger. So effective is it to say that one is sorry that the other is almost irresistibly drawn to looking at the pain the person is supposedly now in, as opposed to the pain that he has just inflicted.

An apology is a tactic designed to place an act of human error, or even negligence, as quickly as possible into the past tense without any genuine attempt to explore or take responsibility for what may have happened. From a strategic vantage point, therefore, declarations of unintentionality sweetened with a show of penitence tend to be disingenuous. Think of a familiar scenario: in a crowded space, such as a subway car, one person is unexpectedly pushed or somehow manages to forcibly bump into another. Typically, there is a brief panic as the perpetrator wonders if the other has interpreted the intrusive contact as unacceptable aggression and is accordingly poised for counterattack. The socially coded "I'm sorry," meant to dissipate the tension over whether hostilities are about to commence, is wrapped in a posture of empathy that, to the degree that it is self-serving, must be false. Were it otherwise it would precipitate a series of remedial steps aimed at concrete reparation (e. g., honest, painstaking inquiry into the extent of the personal injury, cause of the injury, and recompense that may be owed).

This, of course, is rarely done and the person who bumps or delivers some equivalent damage who duly announces he is sorry and who receives the necessary nod of acceptance—that it is understood that only an accident has occurred—is so relieved to be let off the hook that he often promptly and narcissistically retreats into himself. It is easy to see, however, that someone who with good cause has suddenly become anxious that the other may mistakenly view him as an encroacher will wish to withdraw from an interpersonal field that is experienced primarily as negative and fraught with danger. From that standpoint, saying "I'm sorry" is a socially programmed intervention intended to bring not only communication but closure as well—permission to express condolence and almost simultaneously depart. One cannot in this case get away quickly enough and generally hopes one never has to meet the other again.

This can become especially clear if one attempts to imagine the opposite which, in most instances, is fairly unimaginable: that is to say, bumping unexpectedly but seemingly rudely into another, experiencing a momentary panic that an enraged response may be imminent, avoiding an incipient interpersonal minefield through a show of contrition, and then wonderfully discovering oneself sufficiently trusting to explore, get to know, possibly to befriend, the other who seconds ago was feared as a potential assailant.

Usually, in such a scenario, the innocent bystander is equally glad to be rid of the offender inasmuch as both strongly suspect one another of being merely politic and, therefore, wonder what the underlying feelings really are. The person who bumps cannot help but be wary that the other, in spite of his exculpatory nod, is secretly fuming, while the one who was jostled cannot be sure if the apology was genuine or simply a coverup for abusive behavior. At this point the trust level between the parties is probably close to zero. What has happened has triggered reciprocal trepidation and almost instinctively they have colluded to contain the escalation of tension. Since each knows the other has acted primarily out of defensive need, there is often a paranoid sense that the person is hiding his true feelings and a therefore understandable desire to retreat from an encounter in which one does not feel free to reveal what one is really thinking. Instead, one wishes to ruminate in privacy and process whatever emotions have been stirred up.

As a social transaction, the scenario we have depicted can be fairly described as somewhat pathetic, one of the worst possible ways to meet someone. Only when the individual does not feel sorry and assumes the other has most likely not been injured or just moderately discomfited does the presentation of an apology (e. g., "I hope I did not hurt your feelings") become a legitimate bargaining chip, a ploy, or an opportunity to grandstand. When that is the case an apology, which is supposed to be a sincerely remorseful owning up that in some way one has been remiss in one's dealings with another, is actually used as a demonstration of just how exquisitely sensitive and nurturing the person is. Even though there does not seem to be anything to apologize for, he apologizes anyway, as though he is so vigilant that he does not deprive the other, that rather than slip up, he is willing to be gratuitously reparative.

The control aspect with which we are mainly concerned comes into focus when it is realized how difficult it is to respond to someone's apology in any but a preprogrammed way. The apologetic act in effect terminates the transaction. That such termination is usually premature is suggested by the fact that it is rare for people to stop to question, or to feel they even have time to question, the authenticity of an apology. Most often they are too busy welcoming it as a handy tension-reducer. From that standpoint, an apology is a ritualistic gesture of pseudo-reparation, with which two people agree to collude. By contrast, a more meaningful or intimate apology would be only the beginning of a process of interactive repair of the imagined damage one has wittingly or unwittingly caused to the other.

There is thus a substantial difference—all the difference between intimacy and non-intimacy—between pseudo-reparation and a genuinely penitent state of mind. It is worth noting that this difference shrinks completely when the apology is sponsored by a sense of endangerment, such as being jostled by a total stranger, and the person who a moment ago was capable of intimate reparation, no less than the one who was not, will take recourse in a consensually validated symbol of propitiation.

It is a cardinal characteristic of a control game that while it may be emotional, even passionate, it is *never meaningful*. And this is certainly true for those hundreds and hundreds of perfunctory apologies that each of us, in the press of contemporary life, where overcrowding forces people into random and on occasion colliding encounters (physically and psychically), are required to give and to receive.

"I THINK, THEREFORE I AM"

As someone who has worked for many years with gifted young artists from all over the country who journey to New York City to realize or at least try out their dreams, I was familiar with the economic hardship that can often lie in store for them. So it was especially gratifying when Thomas, an aspiring writer, surprised both himself and me by defying the odds and managing to publish the very first book of non-fiction he had ever written. When, shortly thereafter, he proudly announced at the beginning of a session that he had been asked to appear as a guest author on a talk radio show hosted by a man who had previously achieved national prominence as a politician, I was able to observe up close the power of the media to transform the lives of those whom it directly touches.

In the two years I had known him, I had never seen him at a loss for words, but as the days counted down he grew increasingly anxious over the possibility of what he once heard called "mike fright." To ensure there would be no dead air, Thomas struggled to prepare himself mentally by imagining the various kinds of questions he might be asked and then writing down on a sheet of paper the answer he deemed most suitable. When air time arrived, he had compiled ten such sheets of impressive replies and his chief worry was whether he would be able to remember them when it counted. Making matters worse, the interview was going to be live, which meant that the very first time he would be appearing on radio he would be doing so without the safety net of a prior taping, from which potentially embarrassing mistakes could be mercifully edited.

Perhaps sensing his unease, the host, a large, affable man with a leonine appearance whom Thomas later likened to famed trial attorney Gerry Spence, did his best to calm him down. Offering him a can of Pepsi, chatting comfortably, he led him to the studio, a surprisingly small room, from which the interview would be broadcast. In the center of a diminutive metallic table stood a simple microphone about eighteen inches high. Thomas was instructed to speak in a normal tone of voice with his mouth at an approximate distance of six inches from the microphone. To come closer, he was told, would turn the volume up too much, and to move outside of the six-inch radius would tend to make his voice inaudible. Before the program began he was asked to say a few words into the microphone as a voice check in order to determine his natural speaking range. Then a light flashed on a monitor board, signaling that the program was about to be aired. In a gesture clearly intended as supportive and welcoming, the host laid his hand warmly on Thomas's forearm, imperceptibly moved within range of the microphone, began the program with an unexpectedly gracious introduction of his guest, and then smilingly asked his first on-air question.

As Thomas would recount it in a subsequent session, after a moment of brief panic, during which he feared his mind had become a tabula rasa, he self-consciously aligned his mouth to within six inches of the microphone and forced himself to speak at any cost. Out of the corner of his eye he saw unabashed disappointment in the face of his host, who would, he imagined, presumably have preferred congenial eye contact with his guest throughout the course of the interview but who immediately recognized that Thomas was too in awe of the microphone for this to transpire. Yet, afterwards, there was nevertheless a sense of pride and real accomplishment. He had not only been poised enough to avoid lapsing even once into dead air, but he had articulated his thoughts with reasonable assurance, especially if one considered that he was a media neophyte.

What he had found most satisfying, even thrilling—a thrill that did not diminish, but deepened over the succeeding years as Thomas was asked to participate in literally dozens of local talk shows—was the (until then) utterly novel experience of having anyone seriously inquire as to what he thought about a given subject. As his therapist, I had the comparably novel experience of observing what it meant for someone to have his hitherto private views treated with solemn respect by a complete stranger.

I would see firsthand the impact of not only being in touch with one's thoughts and committed to one's feelings, but being asked to stand behind what one says. Although the profound existential value of both knowing and asserting one's idiosyncratic position in a universe of pluralistic ideas seems obvious to someone afforded such an opportunity—which in theory is attainable by anyone, although not as easily as a person on his way to fame—it can come as a revelation. As though for the first time, one is truly identifying with one's beliefs. Indeed, there is a sense in which being earnestly asked to broadcast one's thoughts *forces* an identification with them that is comparatively easy to avoid at almost any other time.

Someone who is invited to speak on the radio, therefore, is automatically challenged to take responsibility for his views to an unprecedented degree. He must package them in a way that is deemed worthy of public scrutiny and then release them to the world. Thoughts, beliefs, opinions that hitherto may have been part of an amorphous subjectivity, intermixed with sense impressions, images, and intuitive feelings, are now—via the magic of a media transform—externalized and objectified. To say what one thinks and to back it up in this way is to accept ownership of all of one's personal history that developmentally preceded the supposedly significant idea. It is not surprising that, analogous to a person who edits a page of writing he knows is soon to be published, one often internally rewrites one's belief before broadcasting it.

An idea that travels in this way from the psyche to the public domain must pass through an intermediate zone where a transformation takes place from one modality to another: from private and psychic to concrete and objective. Often, the speaker can sense the creativity that is entailed as he struggles to facilitate the process. Such occasions, by definition, are rare and one may feel privileged to realize one is actually capable of using one's thoughts to *nurture* the other. At almost all other times, ideas may be used as solitary mental tools with which to picture one's orientation to the world to oneself, to communicate relevant information, but seldom for the purpose of making a meaningful impression on the other.

Thomas's unanticipated appearance on the radio, itself an improbable event, showed me how significant it can be when someone's belief system is resonated with by another person. When that occurs an existential validation of the self is transacted that can outstrip even the famous Cartesian epistemological one ("I think, therefore I am"). Conversely, when nearly everything one thinks and believes is treated as merely one more instance of opinion in our pluralistic society, the psychical equivalent of a political vote, it tends to disable the mind.

To appreciate how desensitizing it can be to consistently experience one's ideological stance to be of no consequence (which is commonplace in our culture), consider how animating it can be when the other (who, of course, does not have to be a radio interviewer) does take one's views seriously enough to pose an earnest question. Suddenly, one's thought makes a difference. The very fact that another is taking time out to explore one's mind is generally an exhilarating experience, especially when it happens for the first time. Furthermore, the asking of a question connotes that time will be allowed not only for attending to the answer, but for processing it and possibly reacting to it. As mentioned, it is rare in the interpersonal domain for such space to be allocated to pure thought. Typically one is content to measure the other's mentality pragmatically and selfishly in terms of how it behaviorally affects one's prestige, general welfare, or security operations, but not as something to be related to in its own right, regardless of its impact. Someone, therefore, who genuinely wishes to examine what the other thinks can seem as though he aspires to make contact *directly* with the thought that lies within and can only be made visible by an act of will.

There is something heady about this—decidedly different from the usual practice of inferring what someone thinks from his behavior and gauging it, narcissistically, as it impinges on one's existence. Openly inquiring of another what he honestly thinks addresses the person's thought in its symbolic (and not interpersonal) mode and thereby endeavors to appraise it according to its representational impact on the public domain.

The fact, however, that this hardly ever happens in everyday life can have an insidious, anesthetizing effect on the symbolic, creative function of the mind. Its omission can allow the control aspects of one's thought—how to use the power of one's mind to manipulate and influence the other's behavior—to come to the fore. As our previous discussion of the judiciary system showed, an especially pure example of this is provided by criminal attorneys whose distinctive competence is to mold the collective opinion of the jury—to bias their minds in the desired direction.

To a great extent a lawyer will attempt to control thought by, first of all, vastly reducing it. Such reductionism manifests itself in a systematic stripping away of contextual richness. Accordingly, a lawyerly argument is designed as a model of logical thought meant to ineluctably guide or drive the thinking of the other to a preprogrammed conclusion. Thus, if possible, it is constructed syllogistically and, if not, then analogically—the best way to control the thought of the other is to *compel* it, either by ostensibly irrefutable logic or by the comparable allure of an almost irresistible analogy.

The hidden assumption, of course, behind the attempt to take charge of the other's mind is that if one did not, if one actually dared to engage the other at the level of autonomous, dialogic interchange, one would be endangered. Lawyers try to justify this by describing themselves as advocates on behalf of their clients of a particular point of view, which is another way of saying they consider themselves and their clients at risk if they were to enter into a free, uncontrolled sharing of thoughts.

What is important from the psychodynamic perspective, however, is that almost every issue or conflict which is centered on human behavior and motivation *cannot* be simply reduced to a question of who can concoct the most logical or analogical argument, and certainly will not be resolved that way. What that means, therefore, is that if someone is to seriously attempt to resolve reasonable doubt in a juror's mind through the tactics of logic and analogy (as lawyers are professionally trained and hired to do), it will be necessary to drastically phase out the complexity of real life.

From that standpoint, an exemplary argument by a lawyer is especially revealing if one looks at everything that it deliberately weeds out: principally, a life-like context that is always to some degree a mixture of positive and negative attributes and always therefore somewhat ambiguous. The evidence of real life, since it does not exist to meet the needs of any one individual or to be used for the purpose of advocacy, to that extent, is *tantalizing*, as opposed, for example, to a man-made argument constructed to be as sturdily unequivocal and persuasive as possible.

In this regard, the issue of advocacy is crucial and points to the differing relationships to reality and what is commonly called truth embraced, respectively, by the lawyer and (his ideological antithesis) the scientist. This is because, for the lawyer-as-advocate, truth tends to have a static, once-and-for-all, irreversible quality. It is something, a state of affairs, a partisan point of view that has been arrived at—essentially, in criminal law the belief that a particular defendant is either innocent or guilty of the crime with which he is charged—and is to be henceforth vigorously sponsored and inculcated in the mind of the jury by whatever means necessary. From such a perspective, truth for the lawyer-as-advocate will be that which has been

completely decided upon in the past and is not open to negotiation or revisionism (unless, of course, it becomes exceedingly
practical to do so, as in the case of opportunistic plea bargaining). It follows that in the hands of the advocate truth will
become either a bargaining chip or a tool and means to an
end, which is invariably to provide the best legal outcome for
the client. When it is necessary that the so-called truth be
revised or changed, as in plea bargaining, then it is done—again,
with the justification that the ultimate master to be served is
the need of the client.

By contrast, for the bona fide scientist, the highest court of
appeal to which everything and everyone must defer is accu-
racy. All else—the needs, wishes, fears, and dreams of the par-
ticipant-scientist—must be sacrificed on the altar to this goal
of the correspondence of designated truth to reality as determined and verified by meticulously, methodically controlled
and endlessly repeated experiments. And, by and large, allowing for the inevitable intrusion of the human equation, this is
what occurs in the practice of good science.

However, because for the lawyer-as-advocate the claims of
truth are only secondary and subordinate to the needs of the
client, a serious dilemma is called into being. For if the primary goal is to inculcate a partisan point of view in the collective mind of the jury to the extent that it is believed beyond
a reasonable doubt, the question arises as to how the lawyer
is to accomplish this when it becomes evident that his relationship to the truth is essentially polemical and self-serving,
lacking in the integrity, impersonality, and dedication that
denote the true scientist. The lawyer's answer, of course, will
be to try to plug up or gloss over the holes in his objectivity
with the tools of rhetoric: never let them see you sweat, never
act less than totally convinced of the certainty of whatever you
say, always mercilessly devalue or outright attack any oppos-

ing thought, expression of skepticism, or counter-argument on the part of your legal opponent.

To sum up, the lawyer-as-advocate tries to control truth in order to serve the needs of his client while the pure scientist endeavors to fine tune the investigatory modus operandi in order to satisfy the criterion of a correspondence to reality. Accordingly, the scientist, instead of appealing to the group mind of the jury, will rely on the quantifiable results of an impartial experiment. And for this reason, truth for the scientist is never fixed and always subject to the reasonable doubt that a single, well-conducted experiment, which flies in the face of the standard view on any given topic, is capable of casting.

It should be obvious that most of us reside between the extremes of lawyer-as-advocate and scientist in search of unsullied truth. At various points in our lives, each of us feels the need to subvert the truth in the service of some pressing intrapsychic or interpersonal project. At those times, the lawyer in our minds will be called into play. And it is because the time we experience the need in our daily lives to lawyer on our own behalf so considerably outweighs the time we feel privileged to reveal the particular truth of our being—which does not, of course, correspond to some external reality, but to an inner idiosyncratic sense of a private self which can never be proved—that control games, based on the illusion that it is possible to imprison the other's thought, seem endlessly to flourish.

THE BELL CURVE

Giselle hated taking tests. With a passion. Maybe it was because her gifted younger brother had managed to garner academic honors so effortlessly, whereas she had been forced to earn every point of every decent grade she had ever received. Maybe it was because, after all, she had an IQ, as she periodically reminded me in our sessions, of "only 110." Convinced that she was intellectually mediocre and devoid of the talent that can convert even the most rigorous of examinations into a potentially pleasurable challenge, Giselle would enter a room in which a required standard achievement test was about to be administered with a kind of manic hopelessness.

Once inside, she would strike up a hasty conversation with anybody who caught her eye. Her goal, in the time allotted before the proctor distributed the test materials and imposed mandatory silence on the room, was to make contact and, if possible, be liked by someone, for she knew that once she heard the dreaded command to turn over the covering page and begin the test she would be utterly and helplessly alone.

Taking a test for Giselle, therefore, was tantamount to devising a makeshift strategy for surviving an imminent traumatic experience about which she had been amply forewarned but from which there was to be no escape. Not surprisingly, the brunt of her energy was devoted to calming herself down, and that meant racing through the test to be set free from the trap she found herself in as quickly as possible. Her tactic was to answer the easiest questions first, in order to bolster her shaky confidence, save the hard ones for later, and either bypass completely the math part, which never failed to panic her, or take blind guesses if she knew she would not be penalized for wrong answers.

Giselle was well into her fifties when she came to see me, but the horror of taking a test, which she first encountered in grammar school, was still very much alive in her mind. Anything that remotely suggested there could be such a thing as a step-like hierarchy of discrete levels of intelligence differentiating human beings infuriated her and she would pontificate against any new book or study which appeared purporting to offer scientific evidence for the validity of psychometric testing. Yet, clearly, she was convinced that her self-assessed intellectual mediocrity was "objective," that her younger brother's academic precocity was real, and that certain people existed whose brilliance of mind was beyond dispute.

As someone who had devoted years toward working with aspiring artists (Alper 1992), I had often been struck by the scant weight accorded to the factor of creativity when it came to measuring intelligence. And this is not so much attributable to the obvious fact that true creativity can hardly be measured, but rather to the reverse—that what cannot be quantified, at least in our culture, tends to be what is not respected. As R. D. Laing long ago ironically noted, it is revealing to see what language *omits*, that is to say, things that exist for which no linguistic term has been proposed. Thus, while there are references and terminology galore to depict the pathetic nuances of cognitive arrest and mental deficiency, there is no phrase that I know of to describe those innumerable people who may fairly be said to be *creatively retarded*.

For me, therefore, Giselle's traumatic fear of being examined was not only reflective of her particular fragility but pointed to a wider phenomenon. Someone who consents to being tested mentally or psychologically is not merely entering or being fed into a computational circuit programmed to terminate when presumably useful information is distributed. On another level, an object-relational experiential one, such a person is also participating in a peculiar kind of interaction.

To better understand the interpersonal significance of the experience, it may be helpful to remember that the aim of the test is presumably utilitarian. According to how the subject performs within the parameters of the test, only a level of proficiency is to be determined. The focus of interest is on performance because of the underlying assumption that there is a noteworthy statistical correlation between the resultant scores and the grade average in school (and subsequently the prospective jobs which require the mastery of those academic skills supposedly measured on the test).

From this necessarily narrow, self-imposed perspective, a test can be thought of as an act of cognitive calibration, but cannot be a reflection, in any genuine sense of the word, of a particular individual's actual achievement in life. It can often be overlooked that the results of an examination are not only uncreative, but they are intrinsically antithetical to creativity. This is because what is being tested for is not something new, an original solution to a problem, perhaps, but something well known, something that lends itself to categorization. The most the test can aspire to is an accurate cognitive measurement of an important mental skill. It is worth considering what would constitute a creative surprise, a discovery for the experienced, assiduous psychometrician. And the answer must be *an original quantity*. If someone, for example, scored an IQ one hundred points higher than anything previously recorded, let us say over three hundred, it would, in the psychometric world, be an earth-shattering event, analogous, in terms of athletic performance in the Olympics, to someone perhaps running the 100-meter dash approximately two full seconds faster than had ever been done before.

Although tests cannot measure creativity, they have no trouble quantifying computational speed or cognitive ingenuity. This can be verified by nearly anyone by merely thinking back to the last time one was subjected to a formal mental examination and asking oneself if there ever was another time in life—except, perhaps, when cramming for a final exam at school, or trying to meet a grueling deadline at one's job involving the lightning-fast completion of a series of cognitively challenging steps—when one was required to think so *quickly*—more precisely, when one's thinking was literally being timed by the clock.

Because we live in a high-tech, overspecializing society, one that relies heavily on the computational expertise of its workers, not much attention is paid to how uncreative such a performance can be. As I have mentioned, much of my professional career has been spent working intensively with, as well as studying, struggling young artists—certainly one of the most creative groups of people in America. Although there has been the customary wide range, from the standpoint of time, in which individual creative works have been produced—some being fashioned with deceptive ease, others with tortuous difficulty— I do not know of a single case where something artistically worthwhile was accomplished quickly, that is, as measured by a clock. Furthermore, while artists often report that significant flashes of inspiration have come and gone in a matter of moments, the fundamental process of working through the technical details of the eventual creative form invariably takes considerably longer. The average can be anywhere between months and years. It is true that in the case of a minimalist art form, writing a short story or a song, for example, something substantial can be composed in a week or even a day—if you are measuring time simply from the inception to the completion of a specific artistic project. But if you are considering the evolution or maturation of a complex creative capability— in writing, music, the theater, or science—then the span of time is at least years.

This is another way of saying that true creative talent cannot be timed by a tester's stopwatch and if one wants to measure it, he must do so according to *developmental time*: trying to be in sync with the organic rhythms and special aesthetic laws of the medium in which the individual artist is working and then trying to understand the dynamics of the interaction between the creator and his medium.

To return to our theme of intersubjective control: because being tested in order to have our performance evaluated is so much a part of our culture, it is not uncommon to dismiss it as an interpersonal experience. So although doing well on a test can often convey meaning in the sense of successfully mastering a necessary personal hurdle, as an experience in itself—to submit stoically to a puzzling battery of disconnected questions—it tends, from the vantage point of the self, to be rather meaningless. And yet, curiously, it appears to reflect the ambiguity and lack of a person-centered structure that characterizes contemporary life.

In the typical test, let us say a paper-and-pencil one, there is an unseen interrogator (the one who authored the test) who asks one mysterious question after another. Presumably the questions are pregnant for the invisible interrogator who solemnly asks them, but it is a part of the opacity of the experience of being tested that one is rarely made privy to the motives of the tester or to the underlying rationale of questions that, if taken at face value, more often than not seem child-like. Furthermore, it is obvious that the experience, although formal, is not dialogic. The author of the test communicates only test questions and nothing about himself or herself. In turn, the subject is encouraged to communicate nothing but *answers*. Interpersonal communication between examiner and subject, therefore, does not really take place between them but *through* the test.

Usually, it becomes apparent that the seemingly fragmented, inchoate pattern of questions must have an underlying code, but it is a code only the examiner is permitted to know in full. In addition, someone who consents to being tested will realize that his personal history will not matter (unless, of course, the test is also a psychodiagnostic one). In the familiar intelligence test, however, deceptively simple inquiries—pertaining to the meaning of proverbs, understanding analogies, extent of vocabulary, facility with arithmetic tasks, ability to think logically—will eventually increase in degree of difficulty so as to be adequate indicators of the scope of adult mentality. From our interpersonal perspective, however, it is significant that although the degree of difficulty may become formidable and adult-like, the form of the questioning continues to be infantalizing.

By that I mean that since the only one who supposedly knows the truth is the examiner, the truth cannot be consensual. It is something, instead, that exists a priori, absolutely. If the subject agrees with the tester, he has given the right answer. If he disagrees, he is wrong. There can be, therefore, no such thing as a bona fide conflict over the truth between them, something that needs to be negotiated. Clearly, then, another assumption of the standardized test is that the tester has access to a higher order of truth. The percipient reader will recognize this as a modern variant of the classical correspondence theory of truth. And even if there is an attempt to psychodiagnostically evaluate the test scores to look for indicators of hidden personality configuration, there is only one interpreter and only one set of interpretations. (Although the subject is encouraged to freely associate to the various projective stimuli emanating from a Thematic Apperception Test or Rorschach card, he is forbidden to interpret his own response.)

The bottom line is that meaning is unilaterally assigned, to be determined by the examiner and not the subject. From an interpersonal standpoint, the subject will often be willing to accept that the actual experience of submitting to the ordeal of being tested is in itself rather depersonalizing, so long as he has faith that the examiner possesses the requisite skill in order to confer a retrospective meaning upon analysis of the resultant scores. An analogy could be made between the purpose of a doctor's stethoscope and the aim of an intelligence test, and it could be maintained that in each case there is a probing for diagnostic signs, in one instance physical, in the other cognitive, that if properly interpreted will yield a telltale profile.

It is obvious that the questions on an intelligence test—what number comes next in this series; this is to —— as that is to——, the meaning that most applies to the following word is ——?—are reminiscent of skills that were deemed most important in the early days of schooling. If an IQ test does test intelligence, therefore, it is worth asking what kind of intelligence? What is the capacity for thinking that is being determined? I think it is fair to say that someone who demonstrates a ready access to an inventory of specified cognitive skills—arithmetical, logical, abstract reasoning, vocabulary recognition, and so on—is evidencing in one form or another *computational* ability.

Another way of saying this is that at no other time is a person required to simulate in his thinking what a computer can do than when he is being tested. It is therefore significant that not only has no one in the history of IQ testing ever come up with a truly original thought, but that no space has ever been allocated for it. It follows that some of the ongoing confusion as to whether a machine can really think must be traced back to the fact that much of our emphasis on what thinking and intelligence are, curiously, is based on a simulation (unconsciously) of computer programming before it was even invented. The standard IQ test in this sense, in its reduction of intelligence to a quantifiable number representing the statistical averaging of an inventory of hypothetical cognitive skills, really foreshadowed the rise of computational thinking which culminated in artificial intelligence (AI).

This may be why at no other time in our lives does our thinking more resemble that of a machine than when we try to zip through the inventory of programmed cognitive tasks fed to us by the programmer/tester (the unseen one, that is, who designed the IQ test). And it might be said that one of the first attempts to create artificial thinking in human beings occurred early in this century long before the emergence of what came to be called AI, when standardized intelligence tests began to be administered systematically to large segments of the general population, such as school children or army recruits.

From an object-relational standpoint, the essence of the test situation is disjunction: on the one hand, there is the world of the tester, presumably rooted in unassailable knowledge; on the other, there is the world of the testee, who is approached as a tabula rasa, knowing nothing, until he has proven otherwise. Elsewhere (Alper 1992) I have described how susceptibility in our culture to the idea of having one's performance deconstructed into a catalogue of part-skills and evaluated at any time—reinforced as it is by early home environment, school years, and increasing specialization of the job market—can culminate in a subtle kind of interpersonal paranoia, compounded of the socially conditioned belief that each of us carries within us a private test by which we can efficiently appraise the behavioral performance of people we encounter and a simultaneous dread that we will be secretly so examined by the other and found deficient, inadequate, or stupid in something.

There are other control games, of course, but these seem to me some of the most important, in no small part because they are so widely accepted. Getting real (or pseudo-real), being stubborn, needy, direct, confrontational, complaining, role playing and so on—all of which can have a profoundly corrosive effect on the chances for intimacy—have become part of the fabric of contemporary relating. As such, they are innocuous-looking but deadly dull defenses against the modern dread of closeness. To a large extent, the covert control that is being exercised here succeeds because it is culturally and institutionally reinforced.

As mentioned in the preface, this chapter has stressed the universality and ordinariness of the control patterns depicted in order to lay the foundations for what follows. The next chapter begins the process of marrying up these control patterns to the singles scene, an interpersonal microcosm wherein they are especially prevalent and therefore easy to study.

2

Strategies of Control

As I indicated in the preface, the position that I take vis-à-vis contemporary game theory is located somewhere between the discrete behavioral series of moves seen in such classic games as "Prisoner's Dilemma" and the more psychodynamically oriented transactions portrayed memorably by Eric Berne (1964) in *Games People Play*. Accordingly, in the present chapter, although by no means do I abandon the phenomenological approach, the emphasis is more on the dynamics of control.

It is worth noting that in spite of the obvious tension between the phenomenological and the psychodynamic point of view, there are important connections binding them, especially as they impact on the person unconsciously caught up in playing a game of control. First of all, to the extent that the phenomenological state of mind, so to speak, will tend to set no a priori limits on what it is free to explore, it will resist reduction, presenting itself as an obstacle to the game player who, inasmuch as he or she relies on patterns or strategies of behavior, must be a reductionist. Games, after all, are composed of rules and rules, in the sense that their definition is founded on exclusions, are intrinsically reductive.

On the other hand, the psychodynamics of human behavior traditionally aspires to find the resultant vector of psychic forces emanating from different or mixed layers of the psyche—unconscious, preconscious, conscious, and super-ego—that impinge upon one another. To the extent that the study of dynamics as applied to people will strive to isolate and trace a

single psychic energy equivalent in its hypothesized transfor-
mations through theoretically differentiated levels of mental
organization, it is reductive. By contrast, the phenomenological approach, which operates essentially on the plane of the
manifestly apparent, is generally regarded as neither psychodynamic nor reductive.

Now, although this is true, especially in juxtaposition with
the classical psychoanalytic intrasystemic point of view, there
is a sense in which phenomenology—to the degree that it seeks
to examine diverse levels or states of consciousness—can be said
to possess some dynamic, and even reductive, characteristics.
It is overlooked that what is normally referred to as reductive
thinking is a purely conscious operation. In fact, it might be
said that the sin of reductionism, if there is one, is that it dares
to gather non-conscious, even non-human phenomena, into a
unitary conscious language and symbolism.

Not surprisingly, the weakness of reductionism is the weakness of the group: whenever one tries to cohesively join together
disparate parts, members, or levels, one must search for the
lowest common denominator. By contrast, genius may be
defined as the ultimate in creative reductionism: nothing seems
forced, there is a sense of flow and an absence of residue. An
insight appears as an instance of genius when it seems so stun-
ningly cogent that no blurry edges or unanswered questions
appear to hover in the background. Connection and meaning
dovetail so perfectly that the recipient has relatively little
desire to modify or resist the new insight, and instead is motivated to savor its esthetic pleasure. When the lowest common
denominator is a language, it will invite the charge that it is
developmentally inadequate. Experts from each respective field
(e. g., biological and psychological) will then be quick to point
out the relevant deficiencies of the proposed common reductive language when it comes to doing justice to the richness of

the observed phenomena and, of course, each side, although pulling in opposite directions, will be right.

A classic example of such reductionism is the ethological program to identify useful behavioral analogies between the fixed action patterns of lower animals and the interpersonal transactions of human beings. To accomplish this, ethology—in order to find a common conceptual language capable of bridging the formidable developmental differences between lower and higher animals—has resorted to the non-verbal and comparatively non-symbolic gestural language that both human and non-human animals share. Although there seems to be little doubt that when ethology stays on its own intermediate, reductive ground (see especially Lorenz 1965, 1980) it can be remarkably successful, it is also true that when it aspires to apply its concepts to the higher phenomenological reaches of human culture that are most distinctively idiosyncratic—the antithesis and natural enemy to the lowest common denominator approach—it sooner or later begins to exponentially disappoint.

The dilemma is this: on the one hand, it is holistically reassuring to find that greylag geese (Konrad Lorenz's famous subject, 1988) and human beings apparently share certain key mating, social, and behavioral strategies; on the other hand, it can seem the profoundest affront to our prized sense of difference to suggest that the admittedly biological similarities between geese and us are in any way fundamental. To be more precise, it is an affront to equate biological and behavioral similarities with existential similarities and we, therefore, absolutely insist on our right, irrespective of whether we are acting as scientists, to reserve the term *person*, with its entire repertoire of multi-layered, rich meaning, only for human beings.

Finally, it may be that part of the conscious repulsion elicited by instances of excessive theoretical reductionism is a defense against the almost universal fear of de-differentiation and regression. Such fear, of course, is regularly fueled by the latent knowledge that the place of the greatest possible reductionism—one that can pile on, overrepresent, merge, condense, and displace not only thoughts but also feelings and images— is no further away than the unconscious (proven to us each night that we dream). And this may explain the nagging ambiguity we are prone to as to whether the differentiation we think we have achieved is genuine or, at bottom, a defensive separatism to shore us up against the dread of precipitate mergings (Phillips 1993). Countering this, of course, and functioning as a kind of natural and welcome enemy of reductionism, is our culturally reinforced sense of normative ego development as a series of stages of cognitive and affective ordering of experience that tend to resist the psychic gravity of the more primitive unconscious layers of the mind.

By now it will be obvious to the reader that I believe the tensions between a phenomenological and a psychodynamic approach are often exaggerated and that there is room for both. If I had to categorize my own position, I would call myself, in Richard Dawkins's (1986) felicitous phrase, "a hierarchical reductionist." My only qualification is that I would apply hierarchical, reductionist thinking to various degrees or levels of conscious organization of experience as well as to the interface between consciousness and the unconscious. And therefore I believe there could be such a thing as a *psychoanalysis of consciousness*, a *psychoanalytic phenomenology* that does not necessarily have to go one layer of the mind down (unless, of course, it wants to), which is another way of suggesting that you can apply psychoanalytic insights and concepts to consciousness without being obliged to pay a simultaneous courtesy to the unconscious. (In the next chapter, under the section "Less Is More," I elaborate on this issue, showing how these ideas are interpersonally and transactionally played out, especially on the singles scene.)

THE SINGLES SCENE

Growing up as a teenager in the fifties, I can honestly say I did not ever recall hearing the word "divorce" uttered in the home of my parents and do not remember a single instance of any member of my extended family, or friends of my family, ever having been divorced. It was therefore self-evident to me when I was married in the early sixties, as I believe it was for my wife, that the marriage would last for as long as we did. So ingrained was this idea of the permanence of commitment that when my wife and I encountered on our honeymoon a very likeable, distinguished, middle-aged man, who in the course of an amiable conversation disclosed that he was not only divorced but happily so, we were both sufficiently daunted as to be unable to conceal the fact that we felt threatened. To console us, our unwanted mentor had leaned forward and in a fatherly way pointed out, "It doesn't mean it's going to happen to you."

In the mid-seventies, it did happen to me and I was forced to admit that I was as single as anyone on the singles scene. But at first I could not understand why, instead of perceiving their state as patently undesirable, they often regarded it, sometimes even with bravado, as an act of self-determination. I had been accustomed to viewing such transience, mobility, and open-endedness in relationships as essentially a failure of the nerve to commit and would normally dismiss them with a flourish of fifties-style moralizing. But something had changed. I was experiencing en masse and up close a broad cross-range of people who in many ways were not unlike myself and who undeniably thought otherwise. Gradually, I was beginning to see that attempting to shore up a demoralized relationship with a pep talk to yourself centering on the virtues of responsibility and commitment had been replaced by the newer concept of working on a relationship.

But what was that? As I was to discover, working on a relationship seemed to mean placing as much if not more emphasis on knowing when to separate from or divorce your partner as it did on knowing when to stay put. The reason for this was that the satisfaction to be derived from the relationship had now moved to the foreground, while the value of loyalty to a particular person had decidedly receded. The result was a curious kind of standoff: on the one hand, there was the gold to be mined by two people working collaboratively and in good faith to enrich an existing relationship; on the other hand, there was so little tolerance for being frustrated, especially in the early stages when the going can be notoriously rough, that even when the necessary chemistry, good will, genuine caring for the other, and honest desire to enhance the quality of the relationship were there, the patience that is vital to its implementation was not.

There is a thematic thread that links up the paradigms for intimacy from the fifties all the way to the nineties. It is this characteristic trade-off which so effectively cancels itself out that it becomes in the end a stalemate. Accordingly, it is not difficult to see in retrospect that time and again something precious in terms of human relating has been gained but only at the price of losing something else of comparable worth. While there is beyond doubt expanded self-awareness and awareness of others, there is also considerably less willingness to put up with undesirable aspects, demands, or intrusions that are deemed exorbitant and unreasonable. While there is increased toleration and diminished anxiety in the face of alternative lifestyles, even ones that are perceived as disturbingly deviant, there is also more impulse gratification and self-destructive acting out as manifested in runaway drug addiction and sexual promiscuity. While there is notably more insight into the vicissitudes of narcissism—in no small part thanks to the pioneering psychoanalytic researches of thinkers such as Heinz

Kohut (1971, 1977) and Otto Kernberg (1975, 1976, 1986)—
there is an unparalleled outbreak of narcissistic acting out. And
while there was the development and appreciation in the sixties of a then revolutionary nurturance, empathy, and humanism, there was also a noticeable and growing paralysis when it
came to initiating contact, a withdrawal from most interpersonal relations, and a precipitate flight into unfettered self-
absorption.

I therefore suggest that the paradigm for intimacy in the
fifties and the rambling chain of its diverse successors are best
seen as well-intentioned but abortive trade-offs that wound
up instead as stalemates, which explains to a great extent why
they are so uniformly unrewarding. Although the kaleidoscop-
ically changing styles of relating have been assiduously chronicled, a rather obvious and fundamental similarity charac-
terizing decades as far apart as the fifties and the nineties
has been basically overlooked: in each period the paradigm
for intimacy, the central model held up for relating between
men and women—although ambivalently adhered to—was nevertheless widely perceived as being ineffective, dying, or perhaps
even dead.

This came to me slowly, of course, often in the form of lessons painfully learned and conferred primarily through the
benefit of hindsight. I had arrived on the singles scene in 1975.
It would be nineteen years before I was able to publish the
results of my own personal and professional encounter with
what has become an enduring interpersonal phenomenon: *The
Singles Scene: A Psychoanalytic Study of the Breakdown of
Intimacy* (Alper 1994).

From the very beginning, I was intrigued by how such simple
ingredients as a broken connection between two people, a sense
of betrayal, of loss, and of being unloved could combine into
something as corrosive as a trauma. Accordingly, the study of
loss would be a major part of the book.

But what was the first loss I experienced when I encountered the singles scene in 1975? As the consciousness-raising groups that had sprung up and were then in vogue and as the almost desperate attempt to revise what heretofore had been (albeit naively) considered traditional, self-evident sex roles made clear, *the first loss was the loss of the paradigm for intimacy.* Twenty years later that loss—due to the repeated failure to replace it with an effective, satisfying substitute—is still in evidence.

In my book I obviously painted with a broad brush. For purposes of the present work, it is enough to say that for all of the above reasons (and others too numerous to go into) the singles scene, as an interpersonal microcosm, is peculiarly conducive to the proliferation (and therefore the study) of control games.

THE FASCIST EMOTION

If anger is a state of mind that often terminates in a visceral motivation, the question arises, what is it that the angry person wishes to accomplish?

Perhaps foremost is the need to abreact or cathart what is usually experienced as a mounting inner tension or pressure to release a palpably uncomfortable feeling. Anger is something inside, just before it is acted out, that is urgently felt to belong outside. While all clear-cut, lively feelings instinctively press for discharge and satisfaction of one sort or another, anger seems unquestionably more insistent. It may be said to be the emotion that aims to get rid of itself through the act of expressing itself: thus in every angry impulse there is also the impulse to destroy the anger that is driving one—to be so as not to be.

Anger is the most impatient of emotions, and may be characterized as an urgent attempt to radically redefine an interpersonal situation that feels intolerable. Thus, for example, one senses that one's associate has subtly but consistently down-graded one's abilities, so now he will be taught a lesson. Or one perceives that someone is not only treating him in an inexcusably rude fashion but apparently believes he can continue to do so with impunity, so now he will be shown otherwise.

Just as one person simply cannot coerce another into respecting him, it is similarly impossible to radically redefine an interpersonal situation in this manner. What happens, instead, is that the target of the angry outburst, realizing that his behavior has been experienced as provocative and not wishing to escalate an already uncomfortable confrontation, begins to act more deferentially towards the offended party. From that point on, the expression of anger can be said to have begun to govern the other's behavior. The message delivered is that if you cannot treat me in a genuinely respectful way—and one cannot on such short notice—then at least be wary, watch what you say and do when you are around me. In a very real sense, anger endeavors, however irrationally, to establish a new code of conduct to which the other must adhere, and it stipulates the punishment to be incurred if one violates it: primarily, further and intensified displays of anger. Pressuring the other to be cognizant of the consequences of disrespecting one's private code of conduct creates the satisfaction that at the very least the other will no longer be able to operate with the safety net of blissful ignorance.

Part of the effort usually associated with the articulation of anger is an anticipation and recognition of the inherent difficulty encountered when one attempts to redefine the interpersonal context in which one finds oneself. Effort is invariably required because (1) in order to redefine an interpersonal situation it is necessary to redefine at least one other person's perceptions, which is not easy to do; (2) due to the urgency, and therefore short lifetime, of anger, it is necessary to achieve the redefinition one desires almost immediately, which is again impossible; and (3) because there is no time for process yet one feels pressed to act, force begins to be used.

The person who becomes angry, who does not at that time experience himself as being understood, respected, or loved, wants the other at least to desist from those actions that are felt to be gratuitously injuring him. The most common method used is to call upon the power of anger—which comes from its menacing mood of aroused, energetic overkill—to constrain the other's behavior. Viewed this way, the redefinition that is the aim of an angry outburst is the staking out of new boundaries, boundaries that are mainly prohibitive: "Do not speak to me in that tone of voice," "Do not ever do that again." Such boundaries are the antithesis of the expansive, nurturing openness that characterizes intimacy. Here, instead, there is the wish to create a negative space between oneself and the other sufficiently wide so that it cannot be traversed.

On the most fundamental level, then, the aim of anger is to control the other through policing his behavior. An outward display of anger can be seen as a personification of one's internalized policeman and may represent the kind of tone, bodily posture, and mode of facial and gestural expressiveness that one believes is most effective in superintending the actions of the other. And since control is the goal, its strategy will rely far more on power than on dialogue. More, in Martin Buber's terms, on an I-it rather than an I-thou interaction.

In a brilliant essay, Christopher Bollas (1992) identifies what he terms "The Fascist State of Mind" in the ordinary person. In view of what we are saying here, vis-à-vis its frequent impulsive, retaliatory, and unprocessed characteristics, anger may be nominated as the fascist emotion. In no small part, this is because it aspires to change the other's behavior, not through nurturance but through coercion and intimidation. Crude though such tactics may be, they work surprising well for a number of reasons. Perhaps foremost is that candid displays of anger directed at another person are relatively uncommon and largely frowned upon in our present society. They therefore can be highly disruptive and a practical goal of anger can be—in order to insure that the other remembers not to repeat a behavior that one finds objectionable—to transform what heretofore has been defined as ordinary and acceptable into a traumatic, and thereby unforgettable, occasion.

Thus anger becomes the great equalizer. By turning the tables and going on the attack, it shocks the other out of his seeming complacency. Now there are two miserable people, which is quite an accomplishment considering there was only one a moment ago. From the vantage point of the person who is angry, who typically feels inexplicably mistreated, it is particularly galling that he should continue to be upset while the perpetrator of the abuse should go scot-free. Retaliation, however, is not the sole motive for lashing out at the other. In a paradoxical way, there is an attempt at being understood, if not through empathy, then through the transmission or induction of a similar mood: that is, the belief that one can only understand something if one experiences it firsthand.

On the other hand, the recipient of the angry accusation of mistreatment, who in turn finds himself unexpectedly thrust into a defensive mode of retaliatory anger, will feel that he has been coerced into living out a mood that he would not have pursued if left on his own. That, of course, is exactly what the other wants, who typically does not take responsibility for his display of impulsive overt anger, experiencing it instead as being externally, willfully, and unfairly evoked in him and who therefore relishes eliciting in his smug oppressor what he senses will be experienced as a comparably incongruent and unwelcome mood. Once again, this time by fashioning a parity of victimization, anger becomes the great equalizer.

Communication through anger may be said to represent a failure to believe in the possibility that the other could imaginatively, symbolically and emphatically enter the experiential realm of the self. Instead of transforming experience into an interpersonal language of sorts, it concretizes it. In most instances, anger reveals itself through sensuous and behavioral self-portraiture. In other words, it makes itself known by acting out. There is wisdom therefore in the common belief that when it comes to the expression of anger, the nonverbal tone of what is said is so much more important than the actual content. (And, not surprisingly, it is the essential proof one points to when accusing the other of unjustified anger: "Don't use that tone of voice with me!")

By comparison with the power of rageful behavior to dominate and hold the other spellbound, at least momentarily, anger works on a considerably smaller scale. More to the point, anger generally works, or tries to work, surreptitiously. It rarely announces or describes itself, preferring instead to repudiate its own existence. So it is one of the truisms of psychotherapy that a patient's ability to fairly, honestly, accurately, and appropriately articulate anger is a reliable measure of his maturity in interpersonal relations.

A caveat: only one important aspect of anger—its capacity or intention to control self and other—will be considered here. The anger described here is not the so-called "good anger"— the ability of a person to stand up for what he believes and does, to defend himself when attacked, to expressively assert himself when someone is refusing to listen, to stubbornly channel his energies steadily in the face of adversity toward worthwhile long-range goals—that every therapist values. Instead, it is the anger that arises from that far more universal situation wherein a person loses his composure, becomes temporarily, impulsively riled up, and typically is aware of an urge to lash out at something or someone. This is the anger—which I

believe is its most prevalent manifestation, at least in our culture—of irritation, frustration and, above all, hostility.

ANGER AS A PARADIGM OF CONTROL

I have spent this much time discussing the phenomenology of
anger in order to show that it is well suited to serve as a paradigm
for the strategies of emotional and psychological control that
are the theme of this book. Some of the basic ways anger assumes
control have been considered: it threatens, it objectifies, and it
creates distance from the other. Although I regard anger as the
most blatantly controlling of emotions, I do not believe that it
is the only force which underlies the need to influence another
person. Certainly other motivations, such as fear or anxiety,
come into play, yet I cannot imagine the enactment of an impulse
to control that does not contain a discernible component of
anger. To this way of thinking, therefore, seduction, which can
be seen as erotic coercion and manipulation, which in turn can
be viewed as non-directive subliminal cueing, also contains elements of anger. (These themes will be examined in much greater
detail and are the subject of a future book.)

NARCISSISTIC GIVING

This is a term I first introduced in *The Singles Scene* (Alper
1994). It may be defined as a defense against the anxiety of
being exposed as someone with an impaired capacity to nurture the interpersonal needs of another by pretending that one
is not only giving enough, but is giving more than enough, in
fact is giving excessively.

Perhaps the most salient characteristic to emerge from a
study of examples of narcissistic giving is the rapid, almost

impulsive nature of the transaction. Typically, a narcissistic-giving response is delivered (and finished with) in a flash. Thus, a woman who has been out of work for three months and who has not heard for over a week from the counselor at the employment agency with which she has registered anxiously telephones for possible news and is instantly told, "Someone will get back to you." Or, as was the case with my patient, a very intelligent, ambitious young social worker who had submitted to his boss a multifaceted, intricately worked out proposal to enhance the efficiency of the agency they both worked for and who—after receiving not a single word of feedback in over six months—finally inquired if it had ever been read at all and was immediately told, "It's right here on my desk." Such speed of reply, of course, cannot be coincidental and what it points to (via omission and reversal) is the simple but profound fact that real giving is a process that takes some time, while narcissistic giving, by contrast, is a non-process, impulsive defense meant to shore up a shaky self-esteem that is notably fragile when it comes to the issue of nurturing another person. Narcissistic-giving responses, as is true of narcissistic responses in general, are characteristically brief, in part because they are tailored for the needs of just one person, and are, therefore, inherently less complicated than a genuinely interpersonal interaction which has to take two people into account. And this is even more true of narcissistic giving, which is usually precipitated by a kind of panic that one is on the brink of being exposed as incapacitated when it comes to empathically addressing the needs of the other—a panic that has the effect of hastening the reply in an attempt to nip the anxiety in the bud by imposing a premature closure on a situation that is anything but resolved.

Not surprisingly, the receiver of such a narcissistic-giving response is often left with the unpleasant feeling that somehow the rug has been deftly pulled out from under him or her. Simultaneously, from the perspective of the narcissistic giver, there is the expectation, and the message is imparted, that the transaction is all over with and it is time to move on. There is a sense, therefore, in which responses such as "Someone will get back to you" and "It's right here on my desk" are designed to deliver the latent threat "Are you satisfied?" This becomes painfully clear should the auditor resist the patently false closure that has been offered and persist in repeating the original request (which then, typically, is greeted with an impatient burst of indignation, experienced by the narcissistic giver as narcissistic injury).

Since narcissistic giving is denoted by an underlying, fragile impatience it naturally strives for expeditious resolution, which it tries to achieve through the strategy of oversimplification and concretization. For this reason, narcissistic givers are inordinately fond of reducing complicated emotional requests, which often hinge on multi-determined dynamic and often unconscious forces to the status of pedestrian one-dimensional questions, as though a complex, conflictual human need could ever be satisfied with the dispensing of prosaic information (e. g., regarding time or logistics).

Other important characteristics in addition to impulsive speed of reply are:

1) *Sleight of hand.* Since narcissistic givers cannot and do not intend to meet the legitimate needs of the other, they use the concrete, in the manner of a magician, as a sleight-of-hand distraction. To that degree, they are not merely indirect, they are willfully diversionary.

2) *Subversion.* They seek to defuse whatever urgency there may be to the supplicant's situation by devaluing the nature of the demand. Thus, there is often a palpable note of mockery in their responses, and a kind of derisive, "So what's all the fuss about?"

3) *Bullying*. They are not above exploiting the vulnerability and neediness of the other, whom they typically attempt to coerce into accepting a grossly sub-par gratification.

4) *Pseudo-logic*. Since they tend to shun insight and introspection, at least in the sensitive area pertaining to their narcissistic giving, they endeavor to reduce complex interpersonal transactions to matters of syllogistic logic, thereby denying unconscious motivation and aiming to boil down thorny relational issues to cut-and-dried questions of conscious problem solving. The assumption, therefore, is that the matter at hand is one of alternative choices to a simple dilemma, and the latent intimidation is that if one does not readily acquiesce to the narcissistic-giving solution that has been superficially presented, then one is either ungrateful or incompetent.

5) *False self*. Since narcissistic giving invariably denies unconscious conflict or vulnerability of any kind and, in effect, relies upon a hastily contrived defensive facade, it may be characterized as a quintessential false self (as delineated by the great psychoanalyst, D. W. Winnicott). This is another way of saying that a narcissistic-giving response is one that is bent upon revealing as little as possible, or, more precisely, the exact opposite of the true self.

WHY NARCISSISTIC GIVING IS
SUCH A UNIVERSAL DEFENSE

Narcissistic giving simultaneously generates pleasure while furnishing a necessary defense. In other words, it is a defensive operation with a secondary gain as opposed, for example, to primary repression, which protects the psyche by helping it to steer away from pain or to head off a threatening increase in anxiety. For good reason Freud considered repression the prototypical defense mechanism. Indeed, certain defense mechanisms (e. g., signal anxiety) owe their existence—being both activated and positively reinforced—to their capacity to foretell situations likely to inspire dread. In such instances, it is easy to see that the chief defensive benefit is a preventive one, arising from the reduction in anticipatory tension and the ensuing feeling of relief that are thereby brought about.

This is quite different from a second class of defensive operations that offer both pleasure and safety at the same time. In the latter category, in addition to narcissistic giving, fall what may be called addictive and sexual defenses: psychical strategies that depend on the peak experiences afforded by drugs or the intense arousal induced by sexual indulgence to act as a reciprocally inhibiting force against an underlying anxiety that is being covertly defended against. To the degree that the defensive maneuver incorporates reciprocal inhibition, it need not be so preventive; anxiety can be more easily ignored, or, when it does arise, smothered. Because of that, a defense of this kind will tend to be more slipshod, impervious to time and conducive to acting out. In this light, it may be seen that part of the reason addictive defenses are so addictive lies in their ability to be vividly and effectively operationalized at almost any moment (in contradistinction to repression, where exact timing is called for in order to bar from consciousness the emergence of something deemed to be anxiety-provoking).

In 1941, the psychoanalyst Otto Fenichel pointed out that people may engage in sexual behavior not because they want pleasure but because they wish to avoid pain. At no time has that been more true than it is today, when addictive defenses have reached almost epidemic proportions. Since strong affect can be engendered with ease through sexual enactment or the ingestion of drugs, these acting-out defenses—which do not require the ego strength of old-fashioned repression that has to muster, without assistance, its own energetic counterforce—

are accessible to almost everyone (where, basically, all one has to do is ride the affective crest of an induced mood).

As a defense, narcissistic giving may or may not be addictive but it is acting out in the sense that acting out always implies interpersonal exploitation of some degree. It owes its universality, as should be clear, to a number of factors: it is operationally simple and can be activated at almost any time; it generally feels good (is ego-syntonic) and thereby provides immediate, secondary gain; and, as an added reinforcing defense, it contains an efficient form of denial: I do not have nothing to give; I have, in fact, more than enough.

INTIMACY-BLIND

In order to grasp the power of the refusal of intimacy—what I term being *intimacy-blind*—to control the other, it may be helpful first to examine the characteristics of a so-called intimate relationship.

Someone, however, who studies the singles scene can look long and hard for examples of intimacy, which, more often than not, is conspicuous by its absence. To understand why this is so, it may be helpful to compare and contrast what is meant by intimacy with the type of relating that is prevalent on the singles scene.

It is characteristic of intimacy that it does not excessively focus on place, agenda, schedule of activities, or fun per se, and that it does not entail anxious, obsessive appraising and reappraising of a prospective partner, but instead commences with a decision that a particular individual is worthy of definite investment. In other words, behavior that may be described as intimate does not begin until restless searching has terminated. It is therefore almost always denoted by an initial phase of digging into a relationship.

Intimate relationships tend to be internal, intrapsychic, and developmental and to that extent there is usually a concomitant sense of epoch, phase, and understandable change. It is typical, therefore, in retrospect, to perceive stages of growth, and for this reason intimate relationships are generally signified by a feeling of historical meaningfulness, in contrast to the atemporal changelessness associated with the singles scene.

People involved in an intimate relationship are more interested in knowing a great deal about only one person, in comparison to knowing what is expedient about many people—a difference that could be likened to that between exploring and shopping.

To the extent that intimacy does not occur until someone, to a greater or lesser degree, has put most of his or her eggs into one basket, it is predicated upon taking a risk. By contrast, relating on the singles scene is predicated upon stacking the odds in one's favor by strategically spreading oneself thin (statistical relating).

Intimate relating is concerned with mutuality, nurturance, and process as opposed to behavior conceived and evaluated as result, end product, or benefit. Although as a process it is infused with unavoidable uncertainty, there is also a corresponding tolerance of the anxiety and suspense over what the future will bring. In contrast to the singles scene—wherein one attempts to control, predict, and calculate interpersonal futures—relationships are not constantly assessed so as to be able to prognosticate, stockbroker-like, their probable dividends.

Finally, intimate relationships are based on trust and aspire toward a position of even greater trust, while relationships on the singles scene rely on a guarded self-interest and primarily pursue security.

The antithesis of narcissistic giving is intimate giving. An act of intimate giving begins with a clear focus on the other's

needs, implicit in which is an empathic reading of the underlying dynamics, which are often exceedingly complex, of the
specific request. In order to have reached this position—the
interpersonal vantage point from which someone can meaningfully and realistically be nurturing in even a seemingly trivial
way to another person—one must have managed, at least temporarily, to set aside normal but interfering selfish needs so as
to be able to invest the required energy. Since the investment
of energy can often be considerable, the individual must be
prepared to spend a sufficient amount of time, and it is therefore a general characteristic of an act of intimate giving that
before it is initiated, there will be a decision that, somehow,
the appropriate time will be found. That is why the antipodal
characteristic of impatience—defined as an irritable attempt to
hurry up a process which one feels, for a variety of reasons,
promises only to frustrate instead of gratify one's desires—is a
hallmark of narcissistic giving and a sure sign of the fundamentally bogus nature of its claim to be humanly available for
someone else's anticipated needs.

It is important to realize that this conception of time is not
measured, as time traditionally is, in standardized segments,
but in terms of being available for as long as it takes to respond in a nurturing way: the clock it goes by is *developmental*.

Because an act of intimate giving begins typically with a clear
and in-depth perception of what is behind the other's request,
it is almost always empathic in nature. It is never purely informational, even when the other seems to be seeking nothing
more consequential than, let us say, the correct time of day,
and the reason for this is that it is primarily concerned with
the interpersonal context out of which the question emerges.
So, for example, if the person requesting time is really expressing a sense of being somewhat discouraged with the way his or
her time is progressing, the other might—after purveying the
desired information—also communicate, non-verbally, an aware-

ness that more is needed than just information. To put it another way, it is a mark of intimate giving that it sizes up and takes into account, consciously or unconsciously, the relational and developmental possibilities that are present. In so doing, it transcends the immediate here-and-now need and anticipates the future.

In addition, intimate giving is:

1) *Congruent.* There is a matching of what is truly needed with what is really being given.

2) *Nurturing.* Although it is characteristically taken for granted in any posture of giving that what is being offered is, of course, going to be helpful or at the very least is intended to be helpful, it is surprisingly rare when help that is given is even minimally nurturing. Real nurturing implies help that is more than patchwork, that is developmental inasmuch as it is capable of facilitating, via a timely and benign relationship, a person's progress in a healthy direction. Intimate giving, because of this, is more often tilted towards the developmental future (best long-range interests of the individual) as opposed to the immediate assuagement of transient difficulties. It is therefore nurturing, and is perceived that way in a sense that narcissistic giving or even legitimate but superficial helpfulness can never be. I think this is borne out by the fact—when you think about it—of how infrequent it is that someone has the experience of being really grateful for the right help being given at the right time.

3) *Meaningful.* Because an act of intimate giving generally strives to reach some part of the core of the other's psyche, it cannot be the meaningless experience that narcissistic giving essentially is.

4) *Reciprocal.* It is characteristic of an act of intimacy that it aspires to make contact with, resonate with, and to be known

by, as well as to know, the other. From an interactive stand-point, therefore, it typically tend towards reciprocity. It is a tendency reinforced by an absence of a power-orientation, which traditionally has depended on the advantages conferred by hierarchical distancing. The result is an intimate transaction whose center of gravity, more likely than not, will be the same for both parties.

5) *Revelatory*. When someone is deeply attuned to what the other wants—in spite of the fact that attention and energy seems directed away from the self—there is an inevitable and significant disclosure of who one is. By its nature, intimacy entails a relaxation and readjustment of one's boundaries, which is prelude to the expansion of and flowing out of the self that is part of the process. To the degree that an act of intimacy entails such an expressive movement of the true self, it will tend to reveal what otherwise would be hidden or at least clouded by normal defensive operations.

6) *Serious*. Narcissistic giving employs a host of strategies designed to trivialize, diminish, shrink, and reduce the other as a means of relieving the internalized pressure people feel to constantly relate interpersonally. By contrast, an intimate interaction is characterized by its intuitive grasp of what is most existentially pressing to the other. Accordingly, it cannot help but take the situation of the other seriously, respect it, and therefore uses language, expeditiously as possible, to express issues of the self, and not—as is common in narcissistic giving—to erect a diverting non-communicative facade of desensitizing superficiality.

7) *Forthcoming*. Unlike narcissistic giving, which relies heavily upon tactics of emotional withholding, an intimate act is one in which a person elects to reduce the psychical distance between self and other in order to be in close enough range to make

greater contact if desired, as well as to be taken in more fully by another who is so inclined. The result is that the receiver of intimate giving often has the novel experience of another self that is approaching or forthcoming but in neither an intrusive nor aggressive fashion.

8) *Binding*. Even a fleeting intimacy can have the effect of inaugurating a bond between two people who previously were not connected, which can later be built upon. In this sense, intimacy is really a foundational glue that binds people together, and is probably the best predictor of longevity in human relations. As an authentic bridge between psyches, it is resistant to normal interpersonal wear and tear and unlike its polar opposite—narcissistic giving—it does not tend, on the first frontal attack, to crumble like a house of cards.

9) *Trusting*. At the core of the defense of narcissistic giving lurks the paranoid fear of being exposed, which in its extreme form leads to the interpersonal philosophy that offense is the best defense, with its concomitant strategy of the preemptive attack. By contrast, trust is at the center, or at the very least at the beginning, of any intimate interaction. To enter into a relationship with another that is in any way congruent, nurturing, meaningful, reciprocal, or revelatory (or possesses any of the traits thus far mentioned), is also to take a risk. In most cases, the risk is not to one's flesh and bone but to a part of the self that has become unavoidably denuded through the act of being intimate. Inasmuch as there is danger, courage is required, and it is no small part of the reason people generally feel good about themselves after they have attempted to be intimate that they know, on some level, that they have been uncharacteristically courageous. The trust that is involved, therefore, is that one, by having the courage to take the risk that is involved in being intimate, will not thereby hurt oneself in some unforeseen way. But trust, being a human attribute,

is not only variable but dynamically sensitive to the interpersonal context out of which it arises, which means there is always a chance that it can seriously backfire. When it does, or when one thinks it does, there is the familiar dread that perhaps one has taken too big a risk, exposed oneself unnecessarily and in fact wrongly trusted. In extreme form, such fears are indistinguishable from paranoia—the traumatic perception that, far from strengthening oneself through a heightened and nurturing mutuality, one has actually laid oneself bare to an untrustworthy other. So although trust, as I believe, is an indispensable constituent of an intimate act, there is a sense in which it is never far removed from and is linked to (if only as a negative potentiality) its inverse, paranoia.

10) *Profoundly personal.* Implicit in many narcissistic-giving transactions is the grandiose belief that efficient and productive impersonality can be a suitable and sometimes complete substitute for the fundamental need of the self to be confirmed in any interpersonal encounter, no matter how fleeting, and that by offering the benefits to be plausibly derived from an impersonal, professional, or business relationship you have thereby delivered something of such value that the need to relate in a genuinely human way can be justifiably relinquished. In sharp contrast to this, an instance of intimate giving, whatever else it may be, is always, on some level, profoundly personal. While it may also be realistic or objective, it is never abstract, dry, or simply logical. It is not politicized. Regardless of the belief system that is held, there is the sense that the person is relating according to some distinctive inner logic that in turn is in harmony with his or her true self.

These are just some of the key traits that characterize intimate giving. There are others that have already been indirectly touched upon. Intimate giving, for example, does not rely upon the tactics of power, and does not attempt to gain deference through intimidation. It pursues, instead, from the other, the respect that is freely given in response to an experience of being nurtured. It does not reduce complicated emotional requests, which may involve multi-determined, dynamic, and often unconscious forces, to the status of pedestrian one-dimensional questions.

It does not employ sleight of hand. It is not subversive, bullying, or pseudo-logical. It is not an agent of the false self. It does not attempt to appear giving by courageously revealing a shameful trauma from the past. By contrast, the intimate disclosure that is a fundamental component of ongoing intimacy far transcends the simple, however dramatic, telling of painful, horrible secrets.

An act of intimate giving, as opposed to narcissistic giving, is a process rather than a one-time, cathartic experience. It is not a confession. It is not looking for release from pent-up childhood traumas. It is not the expression or cultivation of a "victim" identity. It is not melodramatically larger than life, sensationalistic, or titillating.

When conflict is involved, it typically hinges on the capacity, on the one hand, for reciprocal nurturing and, on the other, on the attendant anxieties concerning incorporation, transgression, or dissolution of one's boundaries and the paranoid fear of the dangers ensuing from too much closeness. What's more, such conflicts as do exist will be contained rather than acted out.

Finally, sensation will not be overvalued and pursued for its own sake. Relationships will not be viewed primarily as a means for the achievement of exciting experiences. Instead, they will be appraised not from the standpoint of whether one is getting or is likely to get what one wants but for their power to nurture. The philosophy of Machiavellianism, so preferred by narcissistic givers, will not be substituted for the practice of honestly negotiating and endeavoring to work through substantive relational differences. While satisfactions are, of course, sought, their attainment tends to be deferred and the pleasures they bring are more likely to be the aftermath rather than the immediate aim of the interaction. This is because there will be what Bion has referred to as the capacity to tolerate frustration, normal depression, and the pain intrinsic to emotional development.

An intimate transaction, therefore, is never the product of a hunger for overstimulation, suspense, or immediate gratification, the kind of hunger which is regularly fed by televised daytime soap operas. Instead, it finds its gratifications typically in meaningful discovery, developmental unfolding, and a cohesive sense of process.

Being intimacy-blind, in the interpersonal realm, means simply acting as though there is nothing of an intimate nature to be perceived, responded to, or transacted. It seems to say, or imply, that whatever else may exist or be going on in the universe right now, it is certain that there is no need to in any way consider getting closer to the person who is before you. The effect of this, repeated as it is thousands of times in the daily lives of all of us, can be devastating.

ADDICTIVE RELATING

The great English psychoanalyst W. R. Bion (1992) gave one of the best short descriptions of the psychodynamics of the drug user when he said, "Drugs are substitutes employed by those who cannot wait" (p. 299). It is a description that can be extended easily to a type of interaction predominant on the singles scene that may be called *addictive relating*.

A person who relates addictively to another person on the singles scene is, in an interpersonal sense, analogous to the drug user inasmuch as he or she tends to be someone who:

cannot wait, that is, tolerate frustration; prefers contact with a dehumanized object rather than with a whole person; shuns distance and views a relationship as something to be incorporated; confuses immediacy with interaction, gratification with pleasure, and manipulation with autonomy.

The quintessential example of addictive relating, indelibly associated with the singles scene, is the one-night stand. From the standpoint of intimacy, in particular the avoidance of intimacy, the one-night stand can be viewed as an overdetermined symptom or symbol that represents far more than anonymous sex. It can, for example, be a means of encapsulating or putting a relationship in brackets. Knowing in advance that it will end can be liberating, in a fashion analogous to the patient in psychotherapy who waits until a few seconds prior to the close of a session before really opening up. It can provide premature closure by deciding beforehand when it will end and thereby foster an illusion of control over a process (intimacy) that is intrinsically open-ended. It can create a condensation of coming and going which in effect is a miniature reenactment and reversal of an original trauma of rejection: now you are in control. It can attempt to control what cannot be controlled—the flow of intimacy—by treating it as a behavioral product. It can make transience a cornerstone of relating in order to deny that intimacy is something that builds and grows. It can convert what might be a meaningful engagement into a meaningless activity that has a beginning and an end, thus guaranteeing that it cannot become a process. And, finally, it can act out a manic wish to rush through the natural stages of a relationship so as to bypass any deep hurt that may be lying in ambush along the way, to provide a defense against the inevitable conflicts of intimacy by transforming oneself into a moving target.

Although the frequency of one-night stands apparently has declined over the past ten years—in large part due to the consciousness of AIDS—addictive relating is probably more in vogue today than ever before. To the degree that casual sex has been replaced, it has been replaced by casual relating.

BEHAVIORAL PUPPETRY

I suggest the term *behavioral puppetry* to describe the wide range of controlling behavior that can be observed in nearly every sector of contemporary society but especially on the singles scene. Some of its defining characteristics occur when behavior is conceived of as a product, a package, a measurable quantity, and not as a process or developmental passage; when it is reduced to a unitary force; when it is regarded as a matter of push or pull; when the prospects for intimacy, mutuality, spontaneity, and nurturance recede into the background and the relationship as such comes down to a question of whether one is going to be the puppeteer or the puppet; when struggles for power stand proxy for interrelating and are used, because of the excitement they arouse, to cover up an underlying deadness; when strategic outcomes and issues of winning and losing become a substitute for dynamic interactivity between people; when the world of interpersonal relations is transformed into a Darwinian battle of survival of the fittest; and when the sense of leisure and creative play goes out of relating and is replaced by a premonition of urgency.

Someone who feels controlled by something or someone else can be subject to the paranoid suspicion that if he were more respected, he would be granted more space. Feeling controlled can become blurred with being intruded upon. It is as though there were a telephone or doorbell ringing in the mind that won't stop. And it is because such a person experiences the controlling influences as a kind of low-grade alarm that is constantly going off that it is almost impossible to feel that it is safe to leave well enough alone and allow one's life to spontaneously unfold (and smell the roses).

There are, of course, other strategies of control designed to facilitate the avoidance of intimacy, especially on the singles scene, but these seem to me some of the most prevalent and important. In the next chapter, I try to illustrate these strategies and dynamics of control as they are interpersonally played out, and show how they unconsciously help formulate the rules of the game.

3

Rules of the Game

BEING UNCREATIVE

Denise is a rather proud, aspiring young film director who left her home in Indiana and moved to New York City in hope of finding greater creative freedom. Four years later, here is what she has to say about her experience:

> I am fed up. I don't think it's any easier being an independent strong woman in New York than it is anywhere else. If you're creative, if you think creatively like I do, it's that much more difficult. People either can't or won't understand what you're talking about. Men in particular—the last thing they want is a woman who can outthink them. I refuse to pretend to be dumb, or to give lip service to an idea I consider idiotic in order to make a man feel good so that he might date me. Maybe that's why I hardly ever date [laughs].

Denise makes a point of shunning the singles scene, where she finds it next to impossible to be herself. When I ask her what being herself entails, she sighs as though I have posed a question so needlessly existential that it is impossible to answer but finally says sourly, "Well, it doesn't mean being uncreative."

Denise recognizes that she is different from other people in that she is preoccupied with her creativity. Finding the proper aesthetic medium in which to release it is the dominant theme of her waking life. Like other artists I have studied over the years, she has trouble understanding society's preference for economic stability, nuclear family values, and orderly living. Her own inner world—the one she most prizes—she considers unstructured and even messy but in an interesting way. Not surprisingly, she was one of several artists I have known who seized on James Gleick's (1987) *Chaos* (explicating the emerging science of uncertainty, without which one cannot understand the vicissitudes of large dynamical systems occurring in nature) as a book that lent mathematical respectability to the sometimes perplexing non-linear sequencing of her thought processes.

Although patients, of course, do not generally attribute their sense of interpersonal isolation to a hypertrophy of their creative functioning, I believe that Denise in actuality was only one of many individuals, most of whom are not artists, who experience themselves (usually unconsciously) as coerced by others into being uncreative for the purpose of controlling them and keeping them in their place. If it is remembered that meaningful dynamic intersubjectivity is, by definition, unencumbered by issues of control and power, it may be understood why such attempted disendowment of a person's creative resources is a commonplace and effective defense against intimacy on the singles scene.

This, perhaps, becomes clearer if feelings of being controlled, blocked in her creativity, and put into a box are contrasted with the state of mind of someone who is being truly creative—someone, that is, who is reveling in a moment of inspiration. As a therapist who has worked intensively with gifted artists over a period of fifteen years, I am led to believe (while allowing for the expected range of enormous individual differences) that there are some common denominators of the creative epiphany.

Foremost, perhaps, is that ideas, feelings, images, and mental pictures seem strangely animated, in fact appear to take on a life of their own and to *move*. This is in contradistinction to the much more familiar sense of having to push one's thoughts around like checkers, in step-like cognitive fashion as one labors to meet life's daily challenges. Instead, thoughts now seem weightless, directional, and future-bound. Surprising connections have somehow been effortlessly made and a new meaningful picture of a particular aspect of one's life or private aesthetic vision has emerged. There is an unexpected sense, therefore, of unpredictable growth, and the future has become, at least temporarily, one of possibility rather than of containment or, worse, repetition. (Too often, as Bion [1970] warned, analysts wish to "know what they know" as a guard against leaving themselves open to the unknown.) By contrast, in times of personal creative discovery, you always feel in some authentic way you have just found out something you either never knew before or—knowing it unconsciously—never knew that you knew it. Moments such as these one feels are dynamic and never static. They are hopeful, transformative, and in a curious way, intimate. For once, the hitherto isolated artist feels related and reinforced in his personal identity, with the heady sense he has not only taken an important risk but has courageously survived.

If it is true that the aim of a psychoanalytic interpretation is to make the unconscious conscious, it could be said analogously that an instance of bona fide creativity is also an act of self-interpretation: making the unconscious, the aesthetic unconscious, conscious. From that standpoint, someone in the throes of a creative breakthrough is single-handedly accomplishing what it takes (in the optimum psychoanalytic situation) a minimum of two people to bring to pass: to measurably enrich the interpretative level of self-experience. An important reason instances of serendipitous creativity can feel so exhilarating is that they represent one of the few times when, seemingly, one can provide for oneself what traditionally can only be supplied by the other: the cross-fertilization of a tantalizingly separate perspective. For this reason, the potent creative insight that makes startling connections can seem as though it has literally illuminated the self in a radically novel manner. And the additional fact, that the apparent otherness of the creative inspiration has originated from within, can imbue the person with an eerie sense of unexplained doubling.

THE EXPERIENCE OF BEING CREATIVE

Being creative, however, is much more than a single, dynamic, epiphanous moment in one's personal history or even an exhilarating series of such moments. It is sufficiently experiential to be an object relation in its own right. Accordingly, some of its defining characteristics are:

1) By seemingly being able, magically, to provide in a flash of creative inspiration what customarily only the other can supply—a nourishingly different viewpoint—there is a delicious realization that one has, at least in the flush of generativity, broken free of the habitual developmental constraints of human attachments. Perhaps most satisfying of all, one feels at such peak times that one has found and internalized a way to relate to the self as an object (Bollas 1987) in an unexpectedly nurturing way.

2) Although obvious, it is often overlooked that being creative can be a means of surprising oneself. Indeed, there may be no more memorable way. The heart of the surprise is that

one seemingly finds something inside that was hitherto thought to be outside, and from that standpoint being creative, no matter how strong one's creative identity is, always feels seren-dipitous and to a certain extent usually elicits in the creator gratitude for and towards his creation. An authentic creation therefore carries with it some of the same wonderment (e. g., "*I* was really responsible for that?") that often arises in the wake of an actual biological birth—the baffled realization that some-how the end result, the perceived outcome, has managed to significantly outstrip in terms of integrated complexity the input that preceded it.

3) The creative leap is therefore almost always experienced as *discontinuous*. It is as though the person has psychically jumped to a higher developmental level without having been afforded the opportunity to process the experience upon which the act of creation was founded. Another way to say this is that the psychical gestation of the eventual creative moment to a large extent has been registered unconsciously (like the dream work that, as Freud showed in 1900, antedates the dream). In the sense that what has been now created seems radically dif-ferent from what one was consciously working on just prior to the birth of the creative idea, it can begin to appear that the final product *actually created itself*. To have and identify with such power, which can neither be consciously accounted for by the person nor explained away, is to be in a state of mind curiously reminiscent of the manic individual. It is not surpris-ing, therefore, that someone who is immersed in a creative epiphany will often experience himself or herself as manic but—unless complicated by morbid personality factors—it will tend to be an *objective*, rather than a pathological, mania.

4) The dark side of creativity is that as one ventures into an unknown psychical space, one is confronted sooner or later with the need to reestablish or redefine one's boundaries.

Again, is one breaking apart or embarking on a period of growth? Moving up the developmental ladder or sliding down? Bion's (1987) question concerning the vector of emotional turbulence does not apply only to pathology. What is forgotten in the exhilaration of finding something new in the creative act is that to the degree that one has just embraced the new, one has thereby lost part of the old. If safety depends on familiarity, repetition, and what is reassuringly old hat, the sense of staking out new psychical territory in a meaningful area of one's personality cannot help but be a little daunting. True creativity, therefore, emanating from the core of the person, often carries with it a latent paranoia as to whether the unexpected psychical discovery is going to be integrated into the basic fabric of the personality or, instead, will expose itself as a fifth columnist vis-à-vis the true self.

For all of these reasons, it is difficult to give free reign to and simply allow one's creativity to be, and tempting to yield to its antithesis—the soul-numbing repetitiveness of obsession. Thus, someone even as creative as my patient Denise was not only prone to but positively drawn to obsessive behavior at such times as she felt her mental energy at low ebb. One session in particular brought this home to me, as Denise narrated the weary conclusion to the first date she had had in over a year. Once again she had felt misunderstood, under-appreciated, and treated like an object by a young doctor, a man who just hours earlier at the onset of their encounter had seemed so special and promising to her. Now, drained by the weight of yet another disappointment, she wanted nothing more than to retreat into the cozy sanctuary of her beloved apartment. So, understandably, she was more than jolted when, fumbling in the small purse in which she always kept her house keys, she discovered they were not there. Certain she had to be wrong, she proceeded to thoroughly examine the contents of her purse.

Satisfied this time that they were temporarily missing, she dumped the remainder of her larger pocketbook on the ground and began to systematically inspect every item. Failing still to locate the missing keys, she returned to the small purse to reexamine it. Then back to the emptied contents of her pocketbook, back to the purse, and so on.

Fifteen minutes later, after she had repeated this procedure about twenty times, obsessively examining each item in the same fashion and obtaining identical results, it dawned on her she was in what might be called a searching panic. And had she not, on an impulse, decided to look in a brand new place—the left side pocket of her jacket (where they were)—she was positive she would have continued to repetitively and almost robotically riffle through her belongings on the floor for many more minutes.

When I asked Denise why it had not occurred to her to look in a new place sooner, she was only able to vaguely suggest that something about looking in the old, familiar places—in spite of the fact she soon realized she would not find what she was looking for—made her feel better, which in turn led to further conversation, in the course of which it gradually become clear that Denise was obsessively and irrationally looking in the same place because unconsciously she only wanted to search in places where the object might be found and was refusing to consider places where it could not be found easily (that is, might be lost). When I pointed out this was odd behavior for one so creative, she commented, after alluding once again to how frustrated she had been at feeling unable to be herself with the young doctor, that "sometimes it's a comfort to be uncreative."

At certain times all of us, to a greater or lesser extent, will take solace in the blindness of repetitive, even obsessional, behavior. Some of the comforts of being uncreative are:

1) Since you have already been there, you are unlikely to encounter risks you do not at least partially know how to deal with.

2) There is the illusion that one is controlling time and the future (quite a powerful drive, according to Phillips 1994) and therefore expending minimal energy. The benefits of believing one can predict one's future are twofold: one knows in advance both what pain and what pleasure to expect. (The catch-22, however, is that, since much of what makes pleasure pleasurable is spontaneity and surprise (the eroticization of time), to regulate pleasure is often, simultaneously, to anesthetize it.)

3) Perhaps most comforting of all is that to be uncreative is to be known, to be able to count on having something in common with the next person one encounters, since it is far more likely to meet an uncreative rather than a creative other. On a certain level, therefore, if willing to pay the price, one is afforded a recognizable if minimal identity. By contrast, there is a kind of invisible-man quality to being seriously creative, especially when it does not seem to be going anywhere (such as, for example, slowly gaining public recognition for being a worthwhile artist). A potent inhibition against investing a major portion of one's life in the implementation of a deeply felt, creative vision is the culturally reinforced dread that one may—without receiving any meaningful compensation for the enormous sacrifice entailed—thereby be parting company with the world of people, thoughts, and feelings that one grew up with.

From the standpoint of education and inculcation of cultural mores, since it is far easier to teach someone to be uncreative than to be creative, there is a sense in which society unconsciously exhorts its constituents to be (uncreatively) the same. In fact, to the degree that one's identity (individual and especially social) depends on sameness—continuity not only through time but of recognizability by others to validate, at variable times, an unchanging identity—the motivation to conform will be powerful. Counterbalancing it, of course, will be the basic tendency to forge an identity that reflects what is idiosyncratic about the true self, which by definition will draw on the creative resources of the psyche.

If the psychical forces that go into an individual's identity formation are roughly partitioned into social and personal components, I think it becomes immediately clear that it will be the intrapsychic identity elements, and not the interpersonal or transpersonal, that will be most creative. This is because any initially creative impetus that is distributed through group processes, whether interpersonal or social, almost always becomes somewhat dissipated. The result is that social pressures that are brought to bear on a person's creativity will tend not to be in the service of his or her special creativity. How could they be?

Although this may seem obvious, it is important because it suggests that the sundry social forces shaping the individual will to a necessary extent be antithetical to the expression of creativity. If this is so, and society's imprint is a logical paradigm for the processes which facilitate the containment of creativity, the question arises as to how this will be implemented.

Perhaps foremost is that the person, overtly or subtly, will be rejected if not ostracized in one form or another for being disturbingly different. So painful is it to be rejected, and so powerful is the desire to be accepted that society inculcates, that it is often overlooked that the person is simultaneously being taught that he will be rewarded for not being different (by *not* being rejected). For this reason, aversive conditioning, when it works, tends to make itself disappear: the person, avoiding the behavior he or she is supposed to avoid, does not get punished and, over time, loses sight of what is really motivating and reinforcing his or her habitual desire to (in terms of our discussion) comfortably conform. And, conversely, it will be easy to look forward to and be unconsciously biased towards one's positive reinforcers.

Not only, however, is someone reinforced for not being reactively different by not being punished for it, but he or she is often actively rewarded by being granted the privileges that await the successful group initiate—privileges that typically are not really appreciated until they are withdrawn. The solidarity of the group mind offers a ready-made group identity that is available to any member in good standing. This can be attractive because group identities, unlike the achievement of individual ones, are *conferred*, based on concrete performance and services rendered, and do not depend on the always problematic creative elaboration of selected psychical qualities and aspects of the self. It is worth noting that the sheer weight of group consensus tends to objectify and transform its approbation into something like public opinion, making it the path of least resistance to adopt. The ratification that the group extends for joining the fold, however, can collusively rationalize the intrapsychic fears that invariably arise when one seriously considers being creatively separate.

You might say, therefore, that the group mind depends for its identity on a reassuring assembly of common denominators and that since uniformity, especially uniformity of selves, by definition will tend to be uncreative, so will a defined group. It follows that a group, which will effortlessly outproduce each of its members in terms of quantity, when it endeavors to function as a collective mind, an aggregate being with a supposed identity, to articulate a cohesive group aim, philosophy, or culture, it will sooner or later veer in the direction of stereotypy, if not irrationality. Although the group that is content to simulate a machine can be impressively productive and efficient, the group that imitates a self or mind quickly becomes a slogan-ridden caricature.

Because the cultural differences between men and women can create an automatic field of tension, especially if the intent is to interact intimately, the temptation is to reduce the tension by trying to induce the other (by whatever means) into comfortably stereotypical (that is, profoundly uncreative) behavior. To appreciate how easy it is to oppose, and often successfully thwart, the basic tendency of the self to creatively potentiate itself, it is worth remembering that even in the rare case of creative genius only a minute fraction of the entire psychic structure at any one dynamic moment in time can ever meaningfully be reconstituted (in this context see Konrad Lorenz's [1965] ethological ideas concerning how, throughout evolutionary history, the system has been so much more important than the various components). If it is therefore true that, realistically speaking, only a minute fraction of any one person's psychic structure can be creatively changed, it follows that such change will be more susceptible than the rest of the self to adverse influence. To put it another way, anyone, no matter how creatively driven, can survive at any time without discovering something creatively new in their lives, but no one can survive at any time unless they are retaining *most* of what is old and familiar.

From the standpoint of strategies of control, being or being made uncreative (as Denise protested) is an example of narcissistic giving. In exchange for colluding in the foreclosure of any hope for the free expression of the true self, the person is given the benefits of membership into a safe, solid, and recognizable world. Inasmuch as the technique of intimacy is substituted for the prospect of real intimacy in any such exchange, being uncreative as a control game is also an example of what I have termed behavioral puppetry.

In a truly wonderful recent essay, Bollas (1995) extols the rewards of "unconscious freedom," his version of what Winnicott once called *creative living*. In today's world, especially in the microcosm that is called the singles scene, nothing is easier to corrupt than an individual's potential for unconscious freedom.

STAYING IN ONE'S PLACE

Although Denise was exquisitely sensitive to instances wherein she felt men such as the young doctor were discounting her creativity, she was even more susceptible to narcissistic injuries arising from perceived inequities and abuses of power. From her point of view, the greatest inequity of power in this country could be found in the hierarchical structure that characterized the contemporary world of commerce and technology and the greatest abusers of power were the men who had it. Unfortunately for Denise, she—like many of her artist friends who opted to support themselves with low-level temporary jobs in order to buy as much precious time as possible in which to be creative—existed on the lowest rung of the corporate ladder and was fair game for any male boss who wished to harass her.

When I knew her as a patient in therapy, Denise was working as a part-time telephone sales person, peddling a variety of comparatively unknown products in what is known as a "boiler room." Not surprisingly, she despised both her job and her boss, Mike, a mean-spirited man according to Denise, who early in their relationship apparently had decided that she suffered from "an attitude problem" and was determined to keep her in her place.

Much of her time in therapy was spent ventilating the frustration she felt at having to be taught the lessons of commerce and the reputed fine art of salesmanship by a man she considered a quintessential philistine. It was during one such session, when she was routinely denouncing the numerous inequities of her job situation, that she suddenly wondered aloud if there was any connection between her sense that the men she dated wanted her to be uncreative and her certainty that the men she worked under wanted to keep her down. I said that from the standpoint of wishing to control others and to keep them in their place—since being creative means being able to move freely about in one's privately defined psychical space, which is always subject to dynamic change—there may be no better way than to induce them to be uncreative.

Brightening, Denise remembered a perhaps pivotal exchange with Mike, occurring several months ago, just weeks after she had been hired:

> I didn't in any way try to insult his intelligence but, as I've told you, I refuse to pretend to be dumb in order to make a man feel good. So I say as diplomatically as I can, but I say what I think. And Mike didn't like that. Unless I agreed with every one of his favorite sales tips that he had accumulated over the past ten years and treated each pitch as though it were taken from the bible of sales, I think he thought I was disrespecting him.
>
> So, after about a week of trying to indoctrinate me into his private belief system, and seeing that he couldn't, he invited me into his office for our first official talk. He began by recounting the various milestones that he had to reach in order to attain his present position as supervisor of a telephone sales boiler room. He summarized the prospects and benefits that lay in store for the new employee, such as myself, who manages to make good. Then, becoming very pompous, he introduced for the first time the issue of my "attitude," which puzzled him. He could see that I was a smart woman, so he couldn't understand why I didn't realize that anything less than a 150 percent commitment to my job could take me to the top of this business. Unless, of course, he had been wrong and I didn't really want what everyone else in the company wanted—to be successful and to make a lot of money. Then, with a straight face, he actually asked me the ultimate question—where did I expect to be in five years? Nothing seemed more natural than to give him a short and sweet, honest answer. "Mike," I said, "I'm just here to make a couple of bucks, that's all."

Chuckling as though to humorously disclaim that she had done anything, Denise noted that ever since that exchange a rift had developed between her and her boss, one that was never healed. It seemed to me that Denise could only unconsciously resonate with the mischievous impact of her attitude and her remark, so I said that all she had done, in the space of a single pithy sentence, was to radically define the profound difference between her world view and his, between his almost sacred belief in the value of money, power, and success and her antagonistic point of view that the most she could ever expect from his world was (presumably to pay the groceries and such) "to make a couple of bucks."

Denise, however, was only one of many patients, men as well as women, who, obsessed with the machinations of others who wish to keep them in their place, would take as their paradigm the politics of power as enacted in the daily world of commerce, and apply it to their private universe of personal relationships. If this is so, what is the meaning of this paradigm from an interpersonal point of view, and how is it applied?

In terms of the politics of power, keeping someone in his place might be defined as attempting to *coerce* him into being self-repetitious. Most commonly, this is achieved through pointedly reprimanding the person, in one way or another, for being inappropriately ambitious—inappropriate presumably because the person has not earned the right to occupy the new position to which she aspires (she either does not have the talent, or if she does, she has not yet paid her dues). It is obvious, although important, that telling someone to stay in her place represents the antithesis of the intent to nurture: it deliberately bars the way to further development; it intimates that she has already reached the highest developmental stage she is capable of; or it suggests, that although at some future point she may be ready for advancement, it is first necessary to remain at her present level and continue to maturate.

Typically, the means of keeping someone in her place is to utilize the tactics of power—either the virtual power of being someone's superior in a hierarchical chain of command (the classic example, of course, being the boss who deeply disappoints by refusing to ratify the person's entitlement to advancement) or the interpersonal power that comes from being able, at almost any moment, to radically undermine the other's confidence through the delivery of a well-timed rejection. (The advancement, of course, to which Denise aspired was, in her admittedly atypical case, the freedom *not* to pursue wealth and power.)

It follows that someone who endeavors to enforce the other to stay in her place thereby shows that he is subscribing to the values of a meritocracy and not a democracy. Place (as used in this sense) can only refer to a calibrated slot determined by the amount of social, professional, or monetary prestige one has acquired. If aspiring to a higher place than one supposedly merits is typically judged to be an act of insubordination, it is because this type of place is derivative of a hierarchical pecking order. And, furthermore, while it is one of the cherished ideals of American democracy that everyone is to be able to compete equally for the greatest available success, it is also true that once someone has attained success, he is no longer judged to be equal to those who have failed to do so. It might even be maintained that, in no small part, it is in order to determine who is better in the long run that the conditions at the starting line are supposedly equalized. In other words, by eliminating bias and unfair advantage at the starting line it will be that much easier, when the smoke of competition has cleared, to see who is truly superior at the finish line. Because, however, of the typically American obsessive focus on equality of opportunity at the beginning of competition, it is overlooked that there are few at the end of a competition who are unwilling to declare that the best man or the best woman has won.

In fact, one way to describe a democracy would be as a political system in which everyone has an equal chance to be unequal.

From a psychological point of view, therefore, the obsession with equality of opportunity may be, among other things, an act of unconscious reparation for the suppressed awareness (resulting in a guilty American conscience) that there cannot realistically be across-the-board parity for nearly half a billion people when it comes to individual endowment, whether biological or environmental. To put it another way, even if people do commence life as roughly identical tabulae rasae, the *outcomes* of their life progress—and this is observable right from the earliest measurable point of infancy—are palpably unequal. The sense of unconscious reparation, however, may not only be for the perception that people do not really begin life with an equal biological or environmental chance to excel, but for the realization that there is a ruthless part of each self that does not want the other to be equal. If it is remembered that power is defined as the hierarchical (that is, unequal) distribution of benefits, psychical or material, and the politics of power are strategies designed to capitalize on the perceived inequities so as to consolidate one's position, then I think it follows that a person's belief in power will depend to a definite extent on the intensity of disillusionment with this early ideal of pristine egalitarianism.

Power, of course, is the antithesis and natural enemy of nurturance, which uses what power it has towards the aim of facilitating the other's growth. Moreover, the ability to nurture does not in any way depend on the acquisition of power per se, but is instead a developmental achievement of the self expressed in the interpersonal domain. Someone who, from the perspective of objective power, may be near the bottom of the hierarchical pecking order of a given organization or group, may actually be far more capable of nurturance than someone at the top. By contrast, power, which does not depend on the evolution of the self but on being able to acquire and manipulate essential social leverages, is either conferred or appropriated.

The common justification for keeping someone in her place—that they have not proven themselves worthy of a more responsible or prestigious position—is therefore reinforced by the prevailing presupposition that in a democracy everyone has been given a fair-enough chance to demonstrate what they are capable of. Significantly, the determination as to whether a person deserves her place or not is far more often based on abstracted performance evaluation than on an empathic understanding of the true self. Nurturance aims to potentiate the developmental capabilities of the other, even when the realization of such capabilities happens to outshine the accomplishments of the facilitator. Since someone who genuinely wishes to nurture another will tend to view "place" as a psychical space in which the self can be elaborated, and will not measure, so much as resonate, with the other, he or she will not be unduly tyrannized by the hierarchical view of life, and accordingly will not require the security blanket of obsessive democratic leveling. (From a psychoanalytic point of view, the issue might be said to be does one need or does one want democracy?)

The ambivalence connected with democratic aspirations becomes especially clear whenever one moves from the political arena—which for our discussion includes the politics of power regularly enacted in most companies, organizations, and groups—to the purely interpersonal one. Patients in general, as well as people outside of therapy, rarely talk about a frustrated need for a more "democratic" relationship unless, of course, relationships are politicized and one talks primarily in terms of abuses of power stemming from social inequities of power (as Denise was sometimes wont to do). However, if relationships are not politicized (meaning they are not graded essentially along a power continuum) then inequities are often tolerated, sometimes even preferred, as part of the interaction. Parents do not usually want to be treated as children. Children, except in fantasy, do not want to be treated as adults. Instead, complementarity is often the principal feature and primary glue of relationships: passive and receptive complementing aggressive and intrusive; a need to nurture complementing a need to be taken care of; a need for control complementing a need to be managed, and so on.

It is true, of course, that mutuality is a traditional cornerstone of what is considered healthy intimacy, but mutuality, far from being constant, is always in flux: at any one dynamic moment in time, there is typically one person who is giving either a little or a lot more than the other; one person who is being more misunderstood, deprived, taken for granted, and trivialized than the other. For this reason, the process of working through issues in a relationship is often a matter of recognition and labeling, rather than the actual litigation of perceived inequities. A relationship characterized by mutuality and intimacy is not obsessed with the politics of power, and for a very good reason: it can afford not to be. Someone intimately invested in nurturing the other will almost instinctively respect the person. Respect for the person will reach beyond social proprieties to the self of the other. Respect for the self will, as a matter of course, include respect for the rights of the other. The respect that derives from empathic, nurturing intimacy will be more fundamental and more profoundly encompassing than the respect that originates from a moral obligation to honor the political rights and liberties to which an individual is constitutionally and ethically entitled in a democracy. This is why in an intimate relationship, politics is not an issue. While there may be political differences galore, such differences not only do not divide when there is the glue of intimacy, but often enliven the interpersonal dynamic.

When the relationship is not intimate—which is certainly true of most relationships that are transacted on the singles scene—then power and its politics come to the fore. Simply put: when two people who do not care for or know one another well enough to respect one another interact, issues of whether one is going to control or be controlled will rise in importance. Anyone who is invested in using power to keep the other in his or her fantasized place will most likely derive a sense of the politics of power from ever-proliferating, contemporary everyday examples, and the void of intimacy and meaning underlying it will, at least temporarily, be forgotten. This may be one important reason why the axis of so many relationships one sees on the singles scene seems to be power rather than nurturance, empathy, the elaboration of the true self, and so on. When there is a panicky sense that one is on the brink of being put in one's place or needs to keep the other in his place, the temptation to resort to the tactics of power will be irresistible. There are several overlapping strategies of control (as there usually are) at work when the game is to keep someone in his place, so as to kill off the threat of too much robust life entering into the picture. To the extent that the act of freezing someone in a preordained place is unconsciously justified as being at bottom a necessary if sobering instruction as to where a person fits in the scheme of things, it is an example of narcissistic giving. To the degree that a technique of intimacy is substituted for real intimacy, it will be a case of behavioral puppetry. And, finally, in the sense that brute psychic force, in the typical scenario, is being shamelessly utilized, it will be a salient illustration of what I have termed the fascist emotion.

THE NARCISSISM OF SMALL DIFFERENCES

Although he has dated numerous women in the course of his ten years as a veteran of the singles scene, Jonathan considers Shelly the pettiest woman he has ever been intimate with. If he didn't love her, if she didn't love him, if he weren't so attached to her, if she weren't so dependent on him, if they didn't have such great times together, he would have left her long ago. It is a measure, in fact, of just how much he does love her because he is certain that when she goes into one of her spells, that is when she becomes, according to him, uncontrollably petty, he simply cannot stand her and would rather be with anyone else on earth. Jonathan is quick to supply examples when I ask for them.

I like to keep pictures, sentimental pictures, of women I've gone out with in the past who have meant something to me. Sometimes when I meet someone new like Shelly, who I feel might be special, I'll use these photographs as a means of revealing who I was, what kind of relationships I had in the past, and what I might be looking for in the future. I don't think I'm doing it to show off or make women jealous. No one has ever said that it was a sexist thing, until Shelly.

I'll never forget her reaction. I showed her the first picture of the woman I had just broken up with, Betty. Very pretty and sensual. In the photograph, she's shown with her left arm draped over the top of a couch and her chin perched on her forearm. The picture is half dark, half light, and Betty looks pensive, even mysterious. Everyone before Shelly seemed to agree it was at the very least an interesting, artistic snapshot. But Shelly kind of froze and that look came over her face. Her mouth turned downwards in a tight frown, her eyes grew quiet, and her expression didn't change, as though she were holding herself back. It was obvious something was really wrong and that she wasn't about to say what it was, so I asked her, "Well, what do you think?" and she said matter-of-factly, "She has jowls."

It bowled me over and then infuriated me that she felt entitled to dismiss Betty in that way. I couldn't resist taking the bait. It was true, I argued, that Betty had a weight problem, but I saw no evidence of jowls, and even if she had jowls, it was ungracious to single them out. What maddened me the most, though, was that the more vigorously I protested her pettiness, the pettier she became. Right after the remark about the jowls, she said, "She looks weird, too, like a gypsy." And when I had finished defending Betty against that allegation, she calmly added, "And she has chubby little hands."

What upsets me the most about this is that I can't seem to get Shelly to even acknowledge that she's sometimes petty. I can't shake her from the habit of expressing opinions whenever she feels like it about certain people, which I find inexcusably offensive. And her comments are by no means restricted to photos of former girlfriends of mine. Another example . . . well, you know, I am a little bit homophobic . . . is the way she will off-handedly identify any particular man, whether a mutual acquaintance or simply a person appearing on the television screen whom she happens not to like for any reason whatsoever (she admits this, by the way) as being gay. With few exceptions, every time she does this, I find nothing remotely gay about the guy and I think I'm fairly sensitive on the subject. So I take the bait again; I begin to argue. "Why do you put men down like that? What possibly makes you say that?" And she calmly answers me, "I just think he's gay. That's all. And I think it's obvious." And, of course, when she continues not to admit that she said anything in the least petty, it drives me pretty nuts.

After studying the singles scene for twenty years, I can say that the extraordinary touchiness existing between men and women that sometimes borders on a kind of collective interpersonal paranoia can readily engender states of mind and interactions that may be characterized as petty. What was interesting about Jonathan, however, was that, unlike most patients—who are either unable or unwilling to acknowledge their vulnerability to and hatred of unduly petty attacks—he was ready, even eager, to call a spade a spade.

So what is pettiness and how does it control? First of all, the implication is that by making too much of something, one is either identifying with or revealing the small-mindedness of one's particular point of view. Accordingly, someone who is considered petty is often also regarded as mean-spirited, grudge-holding, and lacking the saving graces of forgiveness and tolerance of the human foibles of others. Furthermore, such a person has probably either been wounded, sustained a loss, or been deprived by another person or by life circumstances, and is taking it out on someone or something in a palpably ungracious fashion. Because in part of their well-deserved reputation for being poor losers, people are often very reluctant to engage them in anything that resembles an honest confrontation, the dread being that if the petty person will not let go of a thing, that if she can make such a fuss over what to others are life's trifles, then when the matter does come down to core issues reflecting on the prestige and security of the self, she will stage a fight to the end. Arguments with a person like this, therefore, often have an unsettling all-or-nothing quality: since everything is at stake, nothing can be overlooked.

MORPHOLOGY OF A PETTY ARGUMENT

Usually it begins quietly and deceptively, often with what passes for an innocent question—"What did you mean when you said ——?"—to which the other finds it difficult not to respond. Soon, however, a peculiar gravity in conjunction with a growing distortion of the reality of what presumably is being rationally discussed begins to obtrude.

When a person such as Shelly is consciously perceived as petty, she is almost immediately discounted as a reliable reporter of consensual reality and put into the category of someone with a chip on her shoulder or an ax to grind. This perception effectively squashes any hope of collaboratively working things out. The petty person is now regarded as so preoccupied with nursing private grievances or sheltering an easily bruised sense of self that the chances of having one's own core needs attended to seem remote at best. For this and other reasons, the demands and complaints of this person are typically experienced as basically unjustified attacks on the self of the recipient. Not only is there an absence of reciprocity but there seems to be a rather bitter determination to wring every scrap of reparation to be garnered. Because petty people in general are obsessed with the urgency of their needs, they often do not realize the power of their negative impact on others. In addition, since they may be aware that what matters most to them is usually considered insignificant, they will tend to underestimate the effect of their actions on others: because their perspective is so often dismissed, they fallaciously conclude that so will their behavior.

For patients who are artists, encounters with pettiness are an important theme of therapy: the pettiness of fellow artists who refuse to recognize the value of their work, of fellow students in creative writing seminars who gleefully expose the amateurishness of their efforts, of acting teachers who sadistically critique the technical flaws of their performances, and of friends and lovers who deride them for believing that one day they are going to be publicly validated. In spite of all my experience working with these artists, I continue to be dismayed at the profound lack of peer group support, nurturance in acting class, and empathy in the contemporary art scene, to which aspiring artists are routinely subjected.

While this is not the place to go into the dynamics of the creative process, one simple hypothesis is that when a predominant part of one's psychic energy is channeled toward a single aim, as is the case with artists, there is a corresponding decrease in the amount left over for the demands of intimacy. Analogously, it may be that when people devote most of their psychic energy toward surviving in the modern pressure-cooker high-tech world, there is also a shrinkage of resources available for intimacy. This means that when there is tension between people, as there invariably is, then pettiness, as the expression of a radical impairment, temporary or otherwise, of the ability to relate, may often seem to be the interpersonal path of least resistance.

In terms of our theme, then, how does pettiness control?

1) By drastically reducing the interactional field to essentially a choice between submission or counterattack, it puts the other on the immediate defensive.

2) It engenders helplessness. The abnormal attention to not merely the details of one's life but to any perceived bruise to self-esteem, no matter how slight, makes it almost impossible to believe that the person can invest in nurturing someone else. At the same time, it is especially difficult to comment on what seems obvious—"I think you're being petty"—unless one feels one is being battered by one uncharitable remark after another. Short of that, the display of pettiness is typically absorbed, silently, like a toxin, by the other, who will then go through the motions of interacting, while waiting for some time alone in which to ponder whether anything in his behavior could possibly have justified such demeaning treatment.

3) Part of the pernicious impact of pettiness is that it is not only the antithesis to nurturance but the nemesis as well of

the ordinary healthy narcissism Kohut (1971) wrote about. It is as though the person has gone out of her way to say the most unbearable thing possible and in effect has held up to the other's narcissism the image that he least wants to see (in the case of Jonathan, that almost all men were obviously gay). It is in fact part of her talent and unconscious strategy to be able to find the most anti-narcissistic image and to calmly announce it as an indisputable fact, knowing how disturbing the impact on the other is likely to be.

From such a standpoint, pettiness can be viewed as a malign way of guaranteeing attention. The target of the pettiness, who up until now did not imagine that such a conception of him could be remotely maintained (certainly not brazenly stated), cannot help but be stunned that at least one person seems to earnestly adhere to it. And since the opinion is unacceptable, sufficient time must be spent to detoxify its impact. It follows that by finding and saying what generally has been unspeakable, the other is coerced into defending his true self. It is not even necessary that the one who is being petty believes what she is saying. Her talent may be more that of satire and caricature rather than of truth-telling, sensing that if she is effectively cruel, the other cannot afford to ignore it and cannot be certain she is not sincere.

Freud's famous phrase, which serves as the title for this section, alluded to the universal conditions under which relatively small (petty) differences between self and other could produce narcissism. It is a short step from that to the person who—characterologically preoccupied with the narcissistic injuries accruing from a perceived repetition of such small differences—begins to reciprocate by behaving in a way that is seen by others as petty. From the standpoint of our theme, what is important is that transactions based on pettiness ensure that there will be no surveillance of the possible deficiencies of the person who is being petty and no danger (for the time being) of connection or intimacy. To the extent that the other is slowly pecked away at, hemmed in, harried, and tied into knots, this is a more temperate, although insidiously drawn out, example of the fascist emotion. To the extent, however, that being petty entails viewing the other as a kind of shrunken, infected dot of almost pure hatefulness worthy of unrestrained scorn, it is a striking example of someone acting as though he or she is intimacy-blind.

LESS IS MORE

A patient, Mickey, is recounting yet another disappointment incurred on the singles scene. The venue this time, he tells me, is the basement of a large church on the Upper West Side of New York City that on Friday nights is converted to a meeting place for singles. People are invited to participate in a variety of experiential, encounter, or discussion groups as a means of breaking the ice, and then are encouraged to pair off and socialize with whoever captures their attention. On this particular evening, Mickey has selected, or been selected by (he is not sure), a serious-looking young woman who at the age of 29 has risen to the position of vice president in a bank. Since he himself is a former stockbroker who is pursuing a graduate degree in industrial psychology, Mickey feels they have at least one thing in common—their ambition. And when, in the course of their seemingly friendly and promising opening conversation, she happens to mention her upset and puzzlement over the recent teenage suicide of a young girl, a high-school cross-country running star who everyone agreed was the perfect student, Mickey senses an opportunity to make use of his new-found expertise. So he begins by alluding to the popular psychodynamic view that depression is anger turned inward, mentions that men notoriously are far more successful in their suicide attempts than are women, suggests that the girl's precocious athletic stardom was perhaps an indicator of an aggressively inclined temperament, and offers the hypothesis that it was this aggression combined with her obvious depression that proved fatal. The banker, who had been noticeably stiffening as Mickey laid out his theory, replies flatly, "I don't see how that follows."

It is clear in the session that this is the pivotal moment in the interaction that Mickey wants to bring forward. He aims to grasp, if he can with my help, why he felt so put down by the woman's apparent reservation concerning the logic of his argument, why he immediately became tongue-tied, and why once again the door had closed on a ray of hope.

"Well," I said, "that was hardly an innocent statement," and I went on to explore with Mickey the possible unacknowledged meanings, for both of them, contained in those six little words: how, for example, under the pretext of a request for a fuller exposition, there seemed to be disavowed accusatory anger on the woman's part, while Mickey, who perhaps sensed that he was being hostilely pushed to defend himself, may have also realized that—since the attack as such was being denied—it could not be frankly and fairly addressed. And, if this were the case, how whatever competition or fight that was covertly going on between them had been effectively displaced from a self-to-self transaction to one of position versus position. Instead of one person being angry at another, the issue now is supposedly that one point of view is right and one is wrong, or that one makes sense and the other doesn't, as if the tension that plainly exists is not between incongruent selves but is really a communicational snafu between sender and receiver. It is difficult enough in such a case when the person directly admits that she has become annoyed over something, but when what is basically a failure of empathy or attunement is disguised as a

communication bottleneck or breakdown in the flow of essential logic, the other has been placed in an untenable position
by being presented with a request that is impossible to meet.
For how can one define, defend, or reveal oneself if one is
restricted to the language of logic and information?

Although it may seem obvious, when stated this way, that it
is futile to attempt to further articulate a self to another who
is patently unempathic, it is nevertheless a common occurrence. People constantly, with straight faces, struggle to answer
unanswerable questions such as: How have you been?; Do you
like the work that you do?; How do you feel about me?; Are
you happy? and so on. To better understand this, it may be
helpful to examine the lure of reductionism: the enchanting
possibility of paring down the numbing complexity of daily life
to a manageable and liberating simplicity, the wishful thinking that somehow one can compress the essence of the self in
just a few simple sentences and thereby connect in a better
way with the other, and the hope that is contained in "less is
more" as a motto to live by.

As soon, however, as the reductionistic program is borrowed
from the hard sciences and applied to the interpersonal domain, its limitations become immediately apparent. Consider,
for example, the familiar situation in which you are speaking
with someone on a subject you know quite a lot about and out
of the blue you are asked to define a key term. It is then, para-
doxically, you may discover that the more you know something
and are intimately involved with it, the more difficult it is to
briefly define to only a perhaps mildly curious outsider. In part
this is because it takes a great deal of work to stimulate interest in a subject for a person who seems to know nothing about
it but who is idly requesting information concerning a fundamental point. Not only is there little likelihood of return on
one's investment, but there is often the nagging suspicion that
the question has been posed, not for any genuine interest in

the subject matter, but as a ploy for deflecting the speaker with an inquiry that cannot be met without some effort, in order to create an intermission in the conversational flow. Although primitive, this is a highly efficient strategy for controlling the other: raise a demanding question, one that the other cannot gracefully decline to answer but one in whose answer you are uninterested, and then sit back and watch.

One of the hardest questions to answer, therefore, is the one that asks you to define, within an ordinary span of conversational time, the work or interest of a lifetime. Thus, upon being socially introduced to, let us say, a brain surgeon, to inquire, "What's it like to operate on another human being's brain?" is to pose a question that is not easy to answer even if indefinite time were allowed and is next to impossible within the context of an ordinary social interaction. This may be one reason why such gross pseudo-questions (traps masking as neutral inquiries) generally are not raised: the person is embarrassed to do so.

This was brought home to me recently by a patient, a very empathic and articulate woman who told me how, after being introduced to a man describing himself as a "particle physicist," she was immediately, if briefly, rendered speechless. When I asked her why, she said it was not only that she was aware she knew absolutely nothing about particle physics, but that she realized any question she might introduce (and there were questions she was genuinely interested in) would be bound to impose an unfair burden on the man: i.e., the extraordinary compression that would be needed to communicate anything at all about the immensely private and technical world inhabited by the particle physicist. While the average person understands this when it comes to such traditionally esoteric occupations or life goals as brain surgery, particle physics, or, I might add, the mysterious domain of the creative artist (one of the reasons I wrote *Portrait of the Artist as a Young Patient* was to make their world more accessible to the general public), it is nevertheless believed that you can ask almost anyone to explain anything so long as certain rules of propriety are adhered to. Such free-wheeling, presumably innocent requests to squeeze into a few key words or sentences the experience of years is, of course, abetted by the information age in which we live, wherein the psyche, to a greater extent than ever before, is viewed as a unique collation of information bits (conceptually reinforced by the popular computer model of the brain). From the interpersonal standpoint, a pernicious equation is unconsciously set up: if psychic experience really can be informationally coded, it follows that the process can be reversed and it can be fed out to an interested party. Furthermore, if the person happens to be a putative expert, in the sense of having mastered a body of specialized knowledge together with the requisite skills to communicate it, there is even more reason to expect that useful information can be effectively delivered.

Yet, as almost anyone who has tried to explicate a complicated concept or subject knows, the greater the gap between the expertise of the teacher and the student, the more difficult it is to bridge that gap intelligibly. To understand this, put yourself in the place of the supposed teacher: imagine trying to explain something you know very well to a self-proclaimed neophyte who has never experienced it. To do that is to try to compress a world of personally meaningful experience into an artificially truncated time frame. You may then, among other things, have to go back to the origin of your own interest, unclutter your mind of each sophisticated advance that would make no sense to a beginner, put yourself instead in his shoes, remember that what you found initially compelling he probably would not (otherwise he would have pursued the matter as you did), and finally remember that what may have seemed self-evident to you may not be so to the other. In order therefore, to answer the seemingly neutral question, the person has to recontextualize a convoluted personal

realm of experience according to the axis of the other's orientation and thereby—by managing to find the appropriate transitional analogy between separate selves—to make one's response
convincingly inviting.

Tantalizing as that may be, the task is even more daunting
when it is the self that one is being asked, on the spur of the
moment, to define. In that case, what usually happens is that
under the pretext of presenting a request for further information, one smuggles in what is essentially a question of meaning involving lived experience (such as occurred in the example
of my patient, Mickey)—in short, a question that can only be
answered with a revelation of the self.

In spite of the fact that reductionism, from the interpersonal
vantage point, leads one up a blind alley, its influence remains
powerful. So it is worth asking, what does it mean to reduce?
In the classical reductive explanation, it appears that two
different time frames and perspectives have suddenly been
joined, as though time almost mysteriously has been abridged
or outright eliminated. The fact that two things usually seen
as separate or very far apart can at a single reductive stroke be
made to fit together can initially seem somewhat astonishing.
And that the reductive connection has apparently endured from
the past to the present, through innumerable dynamic trans-
formations of developmental time that it must have had to pass,
can seem testimony to its authenticity. Furthermore, the very
process of reducing in itself, apart from its contents or results
(in the sense that complexity is being shrunk to comparative
simplicity) can seem magical—not only magical but aesthetically satisfying, inasmuch as the underlying assumption is that
beneath the manifest, puzzling diversity of the phenomenal
world lies a hidden, explanatory unity.

A reductive explanation is thereby *reassuring*, as it seems to
posit a secret holistic connectedness that belies the apparent
fragmentation and chaotic diversity of the real world. By pre-

senting one and only one compelling analogy, reductionism seductively promises to relieve the mind of the onus of having to track down, in its incessant search for meaning, a multitude of plausible connections. The reductive explanation satisfies for the same reason that solving a puzzle satisfies. A natural tendency of thinking is not only to find but to be free to search for solutions. Inasmuch as the appearance of a puzzle can represent a hindrance to the continuance of thought, its solution can offer reassurance that now thought can flow again. Analogously, the reductive explanation promises the removal of cognitive impediments and the prospect of connections galore. And, because different levels of the phenomenal world, in light of their differentiating, emergent qualities, can appear clearly disconnected, to be able to conceptually reduce one explanatory level to another (the aim of every reductive explanation) can seem particularly impressive.

But it is deceptive. The reductive explanation, by focusing on similarities, strategically overlooks or "reduces" emergent differences and in effect tries to delineate only what *has not changed*. It is as though the implicit belief of reductionism is that what is similar is more essential than what is different and what is different—the emergent properties of new systems associated with moving up the hierarchical ladder of biological or inorganic complexity—is somehow just mapped onto an underlying and unifying core.

Part of the impact, therefore, of a successful reductive explanation is that it manages to divert attention from, or trivializes, what is left out or reduced. And what is reduced are not only the emergent properties associated with systemic differences but the very process of change itself: for even if it is true, as the reductive theorist claims, that the similarities are far more empirically significant than the differences, it is a fact that, somehow and for certain undeniable reasons, one level became transformed into another. Why did this happen? How did this happen? And what are the criteria by which it is decided that the similarities are more relevant than the differences?

These are questions the reductive explanation deemphasizes and, by downplaying both difference and the process of change, it manages to produce a comforting illusion of closure and connectedness, as if to say that it is true there are differences and there is change but the more things change, the more they are the same. Part of the comfort of a reductive explanation, therefore, is that it seems to point the way to a lasting truth. Disregarded, of course, is that in order to achieve this effect, it must first collapse time, difference and the processes of change.

It follows that often, upon encountering a convincing reductive explanation, a person feels given to. Suddenly, an aesthetically unsatisfying, incongruous diversity has, at a master stroke, been rendered conceptually whole and simple. From that standpoint, a memorable saying, aphorism, or felicitous piece of folk wisdom can also be viewed as reductively satisfying: a series of perhaps unconnected, contradictory, or confusing life experiences has been deftly placed into a usefully comprehensive context. One can hardly help being at least briefly reassured that so much has been compressed into so little. (On a personal note: while recently reading through Bion's *Cogitations* (1992), I came across the previously mentioned sentence— "Drugs are substitutes employed by those who cannot wait" (p. 299). I was immediately struck by how, in a few pithy words, it managed to distill the essence of the addictive personality.)

In an analogous way, it may be that much of the universal appeal of what is called common sense may be linked to its implicit promise to ignore anything that is superfluous, trivial, or unnecessarily esoteric and instead go straight to the heart of the matter. Common sense can therefore be likened to a bottom line, nuts-and-bolts, pragmatic philosophy of how to live one's life. By concerning itself principally with what works and

has withstood the test of time, by implying that beneath the
bewildering diversity and sometimes structureless phenomenology of everyday life lies an essential core of empirically meaningful experience accessible to anyone, the doctrine of common sense holds out the prospect of an all-purpose frame of
reference.

Analogously, it may be that part of the immense ideological
hold that Darwinism continues to enjoy can be traced to the
reductive reassurance that it provides. It is probably true that
no other doctrine in the life sciences has promised (and delivered) such a reductive unification. Darwin's explanation of adaptive modification—guided by natural selection operating on random mutations—as the summing of small differences over billions
of years manages to link the many millions of diverse species
which exist today under the very same conceptual umbrella.
Moreover, his idea of the common descent of all known species
from a handful or perhaps just a single ancestor—receiving virtually conclusive proof with the discovery of DNA as the one
universal code of life for all species—dramatically connects the
earliest forms of life from billions of years ago to the most modern. Indeed, part of the thrill of reading Richard Dawkins's
marvelous *The Blind Watchmaker* (1986), which tells the Darwinian story of evolution with unparalleled lucidity, is that it
appears to offer a magnificently simple, reductive explanation
for phenomena that seem almost infinitely variegated.

To the degree, of course, that someone feels that a particular reductive explanation in order to work consistently pares
down (as it must) the phenomenal aspect of the experience it
endeavors to elucidate, he or she will find the reductionism
not only not satisfying, but imprisoning.

At the other end of the continuum, however, is the reductionism of a bona fide creative genius such as the great theoretical physicist, Richard Feynman, who wanted to reduce intricate phenomena of nature down to first principles, not for the

pleasure of deconstructing but in order to better understand how to *construct* complexity (build it up from elemental units). In his wonderful biography of the legendary scientist, James Gleick (1992) shows, over and over again, the almost magical joy Feynman derived from his ability to take pristine principles of nature and use them as though they were a child's building blocks. At its best, as was certainly the case with Feynman, reductionism can be thought of as creativity, but *going in a different direction*: it goes backwards (reduces) only in order to triumphantly march forward. Because of that, it never abandons, never loses sight of what it is reducing, by balancing the fleshed-out, quality-rich world on the one hand with the theoretically reduced, toy-model version on the other hand. Far from deconstructing the world because he has lost interest in it, the true scientist simply steps back so as to reapproach it with a fuller and deeper understanding. In his hands, not only is there no desire to shrink, devalue, or diminish the known universe, but there is a passionate yearning to, in an abstract way, form a more intimate relationship with it. A creative genius such as Feynman seems urgently to want to make the universe known to him, since obviously he cannot make himself known to the universe. It might therefore be said that this type of ardent reductionism is an attempt at reparation to the self for the lonely truth that this relationship must forever be non-reciprocal and, especially, *non-intimate*: you (the world) can never know me, so I must compensate by not only knowing you better, but by being able to manipulate and creatively synthesize you. (In this instance, scientific reductionism can be viewed as theoretical regression in the service of the creatively synthesizing ego.)

There is a sense, therefore, in which the "good" reductive explanation strives to *add* to an existing but perhaps impoverished perspective the enrichment of a fresh, unifying point of view and, by making explicit connections that previously were not seen, to enhance, not shrink, the world that it meets. Indeed, language at its best—in its capacity to reduce the experiential universe to a usable set of communal symbols—is a sterling example of a potentially benign, generative reductionism. And needless to say, from a psychoanalytic point of view, the viable interpretation will be reductive only to the extent that it is in the service of the patient's ego, and will (as Fenichel [1941] long ago said) give voice to that which is already struggling to emerge from the patient's preconscious. To put it another way, the non-reductive interpretation, far from inducing regression, facilitates the progressive tendencies of the self.

Nevertheless, ironically, psychoanalysis—which historically set out to show that it was heuristically limiting for one part of the mind (consciousness) to denigrate the value or the existence of other parts (such as the unconscious)—in the past has often been guilty of the reverse sin: denigrating consciousness in favor of the unconscious, as if only an insight which was potent enough to reduce one of the three fundamental topographic layers of the psyche (unconscious, preconscious, conscious) to a presumably lower or more fundamental level, or that could perform the dazzling genetic feat of seemingly collapsing time by deriving a significant piece of adult behavior from its earliest, infantile roots, was worthy of being called psychoanalytic. Although this is not the place to go into it, such unconscious psychoanalytic bias towards genetic and topographic reductionism seems to overlook the fact that there can be many levels and dynamic tensions involved in just one psychic system (consciousness, for example), that to be aware (conscious) is not the same as to know or understand, and that it is therefore possible to apply psychoanalytic insights and principles without being forced to be reductive. It might be possible, as I hinted at in the previous chapter, to conduct a psychoanalysis of consciousness alone, which would be something other than mere phenomenology, and which, of course, in no way would be meant to diminish the significance of the work of the unconscious.

Finally, a point of clarification: although the majority of interpersonal questions, from the point of view of the true self, appear to be reductive in a meaningless way, by no means does this have to be the case. There is such a thing as a creative, meaningful, and even, on rare occasions, what might be called a *Wittgensteinian question* (in honor of the philosophic genius, Ludwig Wittgenstein [1953], and his profoundly original style of philosophizing).

A Wittgensteinian question has been posed when no specific answer or information is sought, but instead a new *way* of searching is suggested that is far more evocative and that cannot be satiated by any single response. The answer seems inextricable from the form of the question: it is the mystery and beauty of the question itself rather than any external puzzle to which it points that is most fascinating. (Among psychoanalysts, it is Adam Phillips especially who has shown himself in his recent books [1993, 1994] to be a master at asking the Wittgensteinian question.)

When reductionism is applied to the interpersonal domain, when there is an attempt to informationally translate or redescribe the true self, the result invariably tends to be noncreative and dehumanizing. What then gets left out or thrown out in such a process of psychical subtraction will be certain fundamental attributes without which it would be difficult to maintain the designation human being: for example, imagination, thought, qualities, meaning, consciousness, experience, and emotion. And it immediately becomes clear that the more of these fundamental attributes that are deleted, the more we are inclined to label the transformation (even if informationally useful in some other tangential way) as reductive in the pejorative sense.

In yet another remarkable essay, "What is this thing called self?", Bollas (1995) goes a long way toward expressing everything that is inexpressible about the self. The person we are talking about here, of course, has no interest in facilitating what is authentically mute in the other. On the contrary, under the guise of innocuously requesting more information, better logic, and clearer facts—bolstered by the philosophical disclaimer that less, of course, is more—an insidious demand for an impossible reductionism is slipped in. It is one of the simplest ways, at least briefly, for effectively tying the other into knots, and it is a particularly striking example of the dynamic of narcissistic giving. By acting as though one wants to sort out an interpersonal muddle, sweep away the obstacles, and get down to what is essential, the sterling impression is conveyed that an earnest desire for greater and more meaningful contact is at work. Thus, the let's-get-back-to-basics approach—which is doomed to failure when applied in this way to issues of the self—promises a fresh start and a future while, simultaneously, silently ruining whatever chance there is for closeness.

"IT'S FIFTY-FIFTY"

It was Joel's favorite equivocating phrase, whenever he wished to escape from the tensions of making even the slightest decision. And for Joel, who was perhaps the most poignantly tentative patient I had ever worked with (whose fascinating case will be presented in considerable detail in the following chapter), making a decision could refer to any interpersonal situation in which he felt unclear as to what he should or might do, say, or especially feel. Thus, if he were sent on an errand from the mailroom in which he normally worked to the xerox room, therein to encounter an aggressive young woman who in the past had been openly contemptuous of Joel, and who on this occasion brazenly preempts his spot at the copy machine, sending him into a characteristic speechless, self-doubting, pro-

tracted funk during which he obsessively wonders who did what
to whom, and I proceed to ask him if he happened to be angry
(an unacceptable emotion in his eyes) at the woman for taking
his spot, Joel might very well reply, "Angry? I wasn't conscious
of that. I was a little annoyed. Was I annoyed enough to be
angry? It's fifty-fifty!"

Over the years that I knew him, I witnessed countless instances of the numbing confusion that could overtake him
whenever he felt under pressure to decisively express himself.
Perhaps most memorable to me was the time Joel found himself impaneled along with eleven other jurors who were to try
the case of a man charged with grand larceny. Two weeks later,
alone in the deliberation room with his fellow jurors for the
first time since the trial had commenced, the jury foreman—
the kind of robust woman who could always intimidate Joel—
proposed a straw vote on the question of the defendant's guilt.
To her surprise (and Joel's) when the jury was polled, eleven
hands were raised in favor of the guilty verdict. Warily sizing
up Joel as perhaps a holdout with aspirations of emulating
Henry Fonda in *Twelve Angry Men*, the foreman, with obvious interest, invited the lone dissident to share with the others
his reasons for believing the defendant to be innocent.

"I don't have any reasons," replied Joel, who had become
panic-stricken, as he invariably did whenever he felt put on
the spot.

"But you must have reasons," exclaimed the woman, who
was beginning to assert herself. "This is a court of law. This is
proof beyond reasonable doubt."

And within a span of seconds, during which terror and confusion seemed to alternate, Joel quietly raised his hand, along
with the others. "Then I vote guilty."

In the session that immediately followed this incident, it
became clear that Joel really did not have any reasons for initially believing the defendant to be innocent other than per-

haps an intuitive awareness of a profound inability on his part
to ever be capable of objectively deciding whether another
human being was innocent or guilty of committing a serious
crime. And, of course, his amazing reversal of opinion in just
seconds was only a spectacular illustration of his habitual tendency to cave in whenever he felt subjected to peer-group pressure of any kind.

Not surprisingly, Joel's characterological tentativeness was
quickly exposed in the pressure-cooker atmosphere that often
surrounds the Manhattan singles scene. Although 37 years of
age when he first entered therapy with me, he was then employed
as an entry-level worker in the mailroom of a large motion picture firm. One of his dilemmas in approaching what he considered an attractive single woman was how to put a spin on the
fact that, while approaching 40, he was, occupationally speaking, tantamount to an office boy. Another dilemma in his mind
was what would he do if he were to ever find himself alone in a
room with a sexually aggressive and demanding woman, given
the sad truth that not once in his life had he ever come close to
achieving an erection in the presence of a woman. But the greatest and most practical dilemma from his standpoint was conversational in nature: if a woman by chance should talk to him,
how would he be able to find something to say back?

Although Joel had been out on only a handful of actual dates
with women during the past decade, and was acutely aware that
he was abnormally frightened of the opposite sex, he nevertheless stubbornly, if desperately, clung to his Saturday night
ritual—as though he felt it was something he had to do in
order to prove there was nothing wrong with him—of visiting a
singles scene venue and making at least a token effort to
initiate contact.

And, on the rare occasion when a woman did take a chance
on Joel, his responses were invariably bizarrely lackluster. Thus,
a typical Saturday night conversational interlude might run:

She: I see you're reading *Sophie's Choice.*
Joel: [enthusiastically, at first] Yes. Have you read it?
She: No. A friend of mine says it's good.
Joel: [beginning to flounder] Yes, it is . . . . [pause] Are
  you from around here?
She: I'm from Detroit.
Joel: [hopefully] Visiting?
She: No. I'm going to school in order to become a dental
  technician.
Joel: [after an increasingly painful pause] That's interest-
  ing. Uh . . . are you good with your hands?
She: I am *not* good with my hands! [turns quickly away to
  talk to another man sitting next to her at the bar]

It was Joel, in particular, who helped me to realize how easily
the simple act of being in the presence of the other—whether
expressing, articulating, or elaborating the self—could take on
the weight of a decision. The decision of how to interpersonally formulate the self could become even more problematic
and vexing than technical problem-solving in the ordinary
course of living.

The kind of decisiveness we are talking about—which seemed
to forever and tragically be beyond Joel's grasp—might be
likened to an unambiguous manifestation of the true self.
It occurs rarely, and usually unconsciously, but when it does,
its aftereffect seems to ripple through the entire being of a
person. Such decisiveness, dealing with core aspects of the
self, almost always represents taking a risk: a commitment
to a course of action will undoubtedly entail consequences.
It therefore feels courageous to be decisive in this manner.
There can also be a sense of intoxication following the realization that a meaningful choice has been made even if the
choice is only one of a preferred psychical direction in which
to move.

To the extent that a person embraces one of a plurality of paths, he closes the door on a world of alternatives. Making a real decision, therefore, characteristically evokes a sense that one is standing alone and in effect has—from the standpoint that one cannot now easily turn back or undo what one has just done without paying a certain price—burned some bridges. Along with that, of course, comes an affirmation of identity. The act of eliminating every possible alternative except one reinforces the belief that the true self is a unique psychical organization with precise needs that can only be met with a correspondingly specific tailor-made solution. Such an act is and feels personal and creative, and will naturally be registered in the depths of the self (standing in stark contrast to the obsessive-compulsive strategy of making a decision by searching for external clues [Shapiro 1965]).

Following Winnicott (1969), there can be a ruthless quality in the manner in which one decides to use an object. After all, one does not merely overlook competing choices that seem inferior, one dispenses with them surgically. Making a decision can be like drawing a line in the sand: this is where I stand; this is where I do not stand (a kind of natural selection of the possibilities of the self, which works by the process of elimination). Since a decision, however, in order to feel like a decision, requires a conflict of motives, and choosing one way automatically entails a rejection of other ways, a capacity is needed to withstand the pressure of the interests of the self that are going to be left unmet. From that perspective, the typical authoritative stance that is often immediately adopted upon announcing to self or other than an important inner decision has been made may be an anticipatory defense against the denigration of the opposing motives and interests, which, frustrated by the refusal of the person to acknowledge their priority, are thereby effectively activated. In other words, as the decision-making process gains momentum, the level of expectation of the competing interests of the self will keep pace, and to the extent that the decision that is finally arrived at is selective, there will be at least a part of the self that views itself as isolated and abandoned. Hope that had been aroused now feels cheated and is easily transformed into rage against an executive part of the self that is perceived as unjust.

It is obvious that the more creative the decision is the more it is implicated in central issues of the self and the less important will be the factor of conscious control. And, conversely, the greater the effort or will to control and take charge of the decision-making process, the less creative it becomes. Although such creative decisions are arrived at, their occurrence is relatively rare. Far more common is it for a person to attempt to exercise top-down control (what I have termed behavioral puppetry) of what is, at best, essentially a spontaneous process. When the element of control is paramount, the person needing to convince himself that one and only one course of action is desirable, making a decision becomes a sterile exercise in psychical reductionism rather than an opportunity and occasion for enriching the self.

So beset by chronic indecisiveness in this regard was my patient Joel, that I often wondered if he were not suffering from a pathological repression of all existential issues of the self. Yet, however much he was tormented by his inability to assertively control himself, he was even more troubled by his dread of being thereby perpetually at the mercy of the other's influence. Without intending to, Joel became a one-man compendium, a prototype in my mind, of what it must feel like to be prone to obsessive indecisiveness, some of its more prominent characteristics being:

1) The person feels intensely pulled apart, almost as though a civil war of the self is being waged. Accordingly, there is a damaged sense and a profound lack of trust in the executive

function of the psyche to undertake the course of action deemed best for the self, especially when faced with adversity.

2) It can seem that the lack of self-knowledge is so great, and the person is so easily thrown into disarray and intimidated by the tension of making any kind of decision, it must be that he simply does not know himself in any meaningful way. The lack, then, becomes a lack of identity, and the inability to resolve conflicting motives is attributed to a failure to achieve a set of core beliefs in the first place.

3) In such a state of mind, it is difficult not to feel vulnerable to ridicule, attack, or pressure by the other. Seeing himself as deprived of a united front with which to negotiate with a potentially hostile world, the person cannot readily trust his instincts. Interpersonal relations are therefore conducted along the lines of compromise and defensive manipulation. Decisions that are made are invariably tentative, designed to be retractable, the intent being to invest as little as possible and to cover all bets. In general, decision making is deferred as much as possible. Since it obviously creates considerable anxiety, there is a strong desire to deny the urgency of reaching any kind of a decision quickly and to rationalize the option of procrastination.

It follows, for all of the above reasons, that someone who wishes to control the other can do so by facilitating indecisiveness. And this can be done by simply rejecting the person outright—for example, the woman who abruptly turned away from Joel to talk to another man at the bar—or by merely withholding encouragement for the other's decisiveness. To subtly question the relevance or to just act unimpressed with what to the other quite obviously carries weight is effectively undermining. This is because even if an individual is self-directed and comfortable with a diversity of viewpoints on any issue that matters to him, there is almost always a need for the other to respect what might be called the existential relevance of what is being asserted. To the extent that a precision or decisiveness of self-expression entails investing oneself in what one says or does—not being in what Sartre (1956) calls "bad faith"—there is a need for the other to be attuned to the idiomatic meaningfulness of the act. To refuse recognition of the existential import of a person's articulate self-expression, regardless of whether one happens to espouse the perspective it embodies, is to dismiss the source—the self—of everything that is being expressed. Inasmuch as authentic, decisive expression necessitates trusting what is to be expressed and is therefore reflective of an intimate exchange between parts of the self and between self and other, the refusal to validate this, as a strategy of control, is an example of being intimacy-blind.

USING

After fifteen years of mixing alcohol, cocaine, and finally snorting heroin, Monica had been subject to the impulse to "use" literally thousands of times. Using, as I was to learn from her, referred to the clear and present urge to track down and ingest the drug or mixture of drugs of one's choice in order to get high. As a recovered addict who had recently celebrated her fifth anniversary of sobriety, and who attended weekly meetings with fellow recovered addicts with almost religious regularity, Monica was rightly proud of her ability to isolate, and then nip in the bud, the desire, no matter how fleeting, to use. Her vigilance did not rest when she did, and each morning she would monitor her remembered dreams for telltale interpretable representations of the wish to use. And it did not exactly take a Freud to interpret such wishes, for the dreams of recovered addicts, as Monica would instruct me, not infrequently portray unambiguous cravings for the experience of being high. What was quite uncommon, however, was for the dream to depict the urge to get high as actually being gratified and when such was the case, so vivid were the accompanying sensations and so reminiscent of its waking-life counterpart that the dreamer would often awaken panic-stricken that she was on the brink of a serious relapse.

From a psychoanalytic point of view, it was of interest that the normally relaxed nighttime dream censor, which can permit at least the disguised fulfillment of a host of forbidden wishes, seems to stop short, except in rare instances, at the satisfaction of the desire to once again get high. The passionate commitment to avoid the traumatic and perhaps fatal repercussions of relapsing that seems to be the principal motivation in the life of a recovered addict such as Monica is continued during sleep in the form of a specially activated nighttime censor.

Nowhere was Monica more wary, in regard to circumstances that might instill in her the desire to do drugs, than when she was beginning to get involved with a new man. As promiscuous with men as she had formerly been when it came to experimenting with interesting-looking new drugs, Monica, by her own account, had had forty lovers in the course of her sobriety. Since she could only be with one man at a time, her affairs, of necessity, were brief, which did not particularly trouble her. What did capture her attention, however, were the patterns of predictable stress points in almost all of her relationships—stress points she had learned to recognize that if mishandled could easily lead to the urge to use: the beginning of the involvement, when she was particularly susceptible to being emotionally swept away and therefore anxious that she was in danger of being taken advantage of; the middle of the involvement, when she was prone to feelings of boredom and disappointment; and the end of the involvement, at which time she could be typically overwhelmed with issues of abandonment.

It was during one such session in which Monica was chronicling her growing sense of dissatisfaction, emptiness, and frustration with her most recent conquest that the phrase *using relationship* flashed into my mind. Until that moment, although I had, of course, noticed much overlap between the life of the drug addict and that of the recovered addict, the remarkable parallel between the relationship of the addict to his drug and the addictive person to the other had not occurred to me.

So what is a using relationship? It can be defined, in part, as the attempt of one person to transform another into an objective and therefore manipulatable source of pleasure. Bion's (1992) comment that "Drugs are substitutes employed by people who cannot wait" comes into play here. Accordingly, someone who feels used in this way might complain of being reduced and trapped in the vise of the other's need to objectify him, being mechanically operated upon, experiencing the other as much more interested in extracting something from him rather than in relating to him as a separate self. Furthermore, someone who is being used often thinks that the other not only feels entitled to treat him as a thing but will resent any effort on his part to act as though he is not a thing.

Analogous to the transaction between an addict and his or her drug, a using relationship is based on need gratification and is, to that extent, transient. When the need is satisfied the relationship tends to be over. The difference, of course (as opposed to real drug-using, in which two users can empathize with each other's habit) is that the high can obviously not be shared when one of two people is to stand proxy for the drug and the other is to experience the stimulation of immediate need gratification. On some level, however, the other knows this and recognizes that something must be given to him as inducement to allow himself to be exploited for another's selfish pleasure, which is why such a relationship is often initiated with a seduction—the user making someone feel good as an unconscious reparation for the secret intent to use him as a thing. From the standpoint of strategies of control, this is an example of narcissistic giving, whose payoff will come after she has procured from the person (whose own payoff is usually some kind of compensatory titillation) what she believes she cannot get on her own and cannot do without.

It follows that the reference point for the user in a using relationship is the particular frustration which is fueling the urge to use. Typically, the user initiates the interaction with the other by referring to a specific frustration (hers or the other's) and quickly improvises a plan for prompt relief. It is characteristic of a using relationship that it is taken for granted that prolonged frustration is a fundamental bane of life and that nothing is more urgent than to bring it to a halt. A corollary of this is that conflict and tension are almost automatically projected onto an environment or interpersonal context that is perceived as depriving. The relationship therefore is distinctively triangular—the apex being the nominated frustration which is begging for pacification—and is denoted by its externality and corresponding absence of intersubjectivity. If the pleasurable, exciting, occasionally thrilling relief of frustration is the prime mover, then the transaction cannot help but be reduced to one of nuts-and-bolts basic survival and means and ends. Strategy replaces interrelating. If every relationship is overlaid, as I believe, with a philosophy meant to rationalize it, then that of the user is pragmatism.

Finally, in a using relationship, *the self is experienced as only a symptom*. This means that behavior is experienced as the manifestation of underlying deprivation. Whatever she does or does not do is viewed as a telltale index of the degree of ongoing frustration. Instead of motivation, therefore, and the drive of the self for expression, what is felt is the *dynamics of deprivation and need gratification*. Any interpersonal meaning, other than the opportunistically pressing one of escaping the impingement of circumstances seen as traumatically thwarting, fades into the background.

On the other hand, once the sense of a deprived self is temporarily sated with pseudo-rewards, the intrinsic meaninglessness of organizing one's life, as the user does, around the avoidance or obsessive control of feelings of psychic destitution becomes evident in the predictable aftermath known as crashing, which can be existential as well as physiological, that is, a crash of meaning.

For all of these reasons, the identity of each party in a using relationship does not need to come into play and can be readily ignored. The person can be intimacy-blind with impunity if he or she chooses. But as a strategy of control it is an outstanding example of what I have termed addictive relating.

BEING DEFENSIVE

A patient, known to himself and to me to be highly sensitive to perceived criticism, goes to a singles place and meets up with an attractive woman who happens to be in the same advertising business that he is in. Encouraged that he has perhaps found at least a professional soulmate, he decides to open up about a recent occurrence at work that has distressed him, recounting how, in response to a possible new client's request for further relevant information, he had dashed off a specially prepared marketing package, which he naturally assumed would be delivered by UPS in a matter of days but which, to his subsequent chagrin, was mailed fourth class and did not arrive for several weeks. The woman, who at first had listened attentively, now apparently was reacting to the story personally, and icily retorted, "At my place, we always send it UPS!"

Notwithstanding the fact that my patient is hypersensitive to rebuffs, it is easy to see why he felt effectively dismantled by the woman's response. In a patent effort to draw closer to her, he had started from the comparatively safe professional ground they shared in common, and proceeded to unburden himself of what he experienced as a deflating lack of support from whoever was responsible for efficiently mailing out important marketing packages. As a consequence, he had suffered a minor blow to his professional self-esteem and plainly was looking for some empathy with perhaps a dash of nurturance thrown in. On another level—given that the context of the interaction was a singles scene meeting place—he was making at least a tentative effort toward being more intimate with an interesting-looking woman he had just met.

Unfortunately, as my patient had noted, the woman, for whatever reason, had reacted to his narrative of a distressing incident that had recently occurred on his job as though he had somehow slighted her. Perhaps, my patient had subsequently wondered, the woman had interpreted what he had said as a broadside attack on the advertising industry, which thereby implicated her own firm and, by association, herself as well?

From the perspective of intimacy, this simple interaction, which probably occurs in one form or another thousands of times in the lives of each of us, can serve as a paradigm of what can go wrong. A man, under the guise of revealing a personal slight incurred on his job, makes an overture to a woman for some more-than-superficial contact. The woman is either unable, unwilling, or just not prepared to reciprocate. Whatever else she wants, she does not wish for greater closeness with this particular man at this moment in time.

So what does she do? She becomes defensive. That is to say, she transforms, or unconsciously interprets, what he says and does as obliquely or directly critical of something to do with some aspect of her life. Now she does not have to deal with the meaning of what the other seems struggling to express: in fact, since she has relegated it to the category of hostile behavior, she can either ignore it entirely or respond in kind.

Someone who becomes defensive in this way negatively frames what might, in different circumstances, be an occasion for intersubjectivity. Defining the relationship as adversarial eliminates any plausible need for cooperation, mutuality, or genuine contact. Inasmuch as the act of being defensive usually stimulates a reciprocal guardedness in the other, it almost automatically guarantees that a certain interpersonal distance will be established. And even if the other, instead of passively being driven into a retaliative withdrawal, takes offense and chooses to close ground in order to attack, the contact (of battle) that may ensue will be combative rather than intimate.

It is considerably easier to provoke someone into a defensive posture than to engage him or her intimately. And this is because intimacy—by dint of its complex, precarious nature, the fact that so many things can go wrong, that one is opening oneself up to rejection, and that therefore the risk of getting hurt is high—is especially fragile at its inception (in stark contrast to its ability, when maturely developed, to form a powerful bond). *Intimacy, at its birth, needs to be nurtured.* The reverse of this, of course, is that it is easy to kill in its infancy. (Think of someone you take notice of in a room for the first time, whom you are interested in and would like to make contact with, but who, upon seeing you approach, turns pointedly and coldly away. It is then almost impossible to ever think seriously of approaching again.)

By contrast, defensiveness is easy to elicit and to keep going if one wants to. Being mistrustful and staying on one's guard can be an almost automatic and repetitive way of relating (or not relating) and as such requires minimal investment or foresight. Furthermore, defensiveness—if it does not cause embarrassment by calling attention to itself—can be reassuring in the sense that at least one is not amiss when it comes to protecting one's interests. Just in case someone is thinking of taking advantage, the defensive posture is quite an effective deterrent: putting him on notice that he is being watched, and sending the message that if he does try to violate one's boundaries, one is prepared to fight. And should advantage already have been taken, then the stance of critical vigilance acts as necessary damage control. Defensiveness is easy, therefore, because no new risk is involved. It tends to eliminate the future by treating it as the past, and it attenuates existing threats. Inasmuch as it falsely reassures by sending a message to the self—at least I am nobody's fool—it is an instance of narcissistic giving.

It should be obvious that being defensive, which invariably increases interpersonal distance, is the antithesis of being intimate. Distance, however, makes sense from the standpoint of the defensive state of mind because it seems to lend perspective, to provide needed space and a vantage point from which a suspect other can be safely scrutinized and objectively appraised; the person endeavors to move beyond the range of danger of contamination by contact.

Being defensively adversarial therefore redefines an interpersonal context so as to effectively ward off an occasion for intimacy. In order, however, to keep the undercurrent of adversarial tension from escalating, it is often displaced—as the example of my patient shows—so that the apparent disagreement is not between people or selves but between differing points of view. The ambivalence thus afforded represents a handy safety net: should the person, such as my patient, who suddenly finds himself the target of the other's defensiveness protest by saying, "I didn't mean anything personal—I wasn't talking about you or your company," the other can quite plausibly respond, "And I didn't take it personally—I was only talking about my company's policy."

"I CAN'T AFFORD IT"

There is a variant of narcissistic giving which may be called *narcissistic honesty*: the attempt to deflect expected criticism for an unconsciously perceived failing by brazenly admitting it, as if to thereby indicate that, far from being ashamed, one is actually proud of what one has often been accused of. Thus, as can be often noted, someone who is known to be hostile and insensitive will defend himself by volunteering, "Yes, I am blunt."

When the deficit in question happens to be an incapacity to relate or to be intimate, narcissistic honesty is a popular defense. Such was the case when the boyfriend of a patient, who for several months had acted as though he were steadily falling in love, suddenly announced, "When I first met you I really thought this could develop into something romantic. But it hasn't, and I don't want to be in that kind of relationship anymore."

In the session, the woman cries bitterly, freely expresses the various levels of her disappointment, and in so doing gives a good picture of what it feels like to have the relational rug pulled out from under one's feet. It hurts not only because so much has been taken away in such a short time, but because, perhaps even more unfairly, no transitional space has been provided in which to make a desperately needed adjustment. In relationship terms, the person has sustained a quantum drop. Making it all the more powerful is the fact that the other apparently is denying any responsibility for the psychic wreckage he has left in the wake of his tranquil message of doom. Radical withdrawal such as this can be almost unbearable because it takes a relationship in which two people are seemingly meaningfully engaged and unilaterally redefines it without allowing the other the slightest say or input. There is then, in addition to feelings of resentment, a chilling sense of what at various times in our lives each of us experiences as "They have the power."

By denying, as my patient's boyfriend seemed to do, that one is effectively moving out of the interpersonal domain (by radically withdrawing), one simultaneously denies the right of the other to protest and to try to assuage inescapable feelings of abandonment. Typically, the denial is in the form of insisting that the retreat to a more distant relationship is simply the outcome of a natural and therefore healthy process—human affiliations, so it goes, wax and wane like everything else—and does not therefore signal (as I believe it does) a sudden rupture in an already fragile ability to be intimate. Accordingly, a second-tier denial on the part of someone who is engaged in narcissistic honesty is to defiantly claim, should the callousness of his behavior be called into question, that the other is trying to curtail his right to self-determination.

Here is another example, a personal and professional one. A woman, a 30-year-old painter, who has been in therapy with me for a year, matter-of-factly announces toward the end of the session that she will be unable to keep her appointment the following week. When I offer to reschedule the session for her at a mutually convenient time, she looks at me quizzically. "Oh, is that your policy? I have to make it up?" And with that my heart sinks as I realize that the woman who I thought was more or less vitally connected to the therapeutic process, and the therapeutic relationship that I definitely believed was generatively moving along, are no longer present. So I somewhat nervously remind her of my policy regarding makeups by which she had agreed to abide a year ago, and, noting that she appears unruffled at my restatement, proceed to reschedule the appointment. But I am not surprised on the day of the makeup to receive her telephone call and to be joined in the following conversation.

She: I know this is short notice, but I've been thinking
   things over.
Me: [trying to hide the fact that I am immediately crest-
   fallen] Yes?
She: I can't really afford to come in for an extra session
   this week. [pause]
Me: Well, you can owe it.
She: It's not just that. I've been thinking that maybe I
   can't afford therapy at this point in my life. I realize
   your rates are fair, but I feel it would be best for me to
   take a break.
Me: Well, how about coming in and discussing it one last
   time?
She: Why? What would I talk about?
Me: [taken aback once more] Sometimes important
   things come up in the last session that can make it
   worthwhile. Also, it's a more personal way of saying
   good-bye.
She: Do I have to? Can't I do it on the telephone?
Me: You can do it on the telephone. But tell me, as I
   really am surprised, did something happen in the
   therapy, did I say or do anything that upset you and
   made you want to stop?
She: [in a calm, dead voice] No. I just can't afford it.

And in a trice a relationship that I had considered to be
solidly, mutually, and therapeutically enriching, was over.
Without going further into the etiology and dynamics of her
departure, I want to focus on the simple but enormous power
the act of radical withdrawal has to alter the other. For days
after this episode, I suffered from a recurrent, painful, forlorn
sense of almost total, inexplicable dismissal, a loss of something
quite valuable that I had internalized, and an unwanted

appreciation of the capacity of the other to engender feelings of powerlessness in me.

Although it goes with the territory of being a therapist that one is subject to being summarily dismissed at any time by any patient, I believe there is another, deeper reason for how therapy can unwittingly provide a facilitating environment for the wholesale flight from intimacy, one that goes to the heart of the paradoxical nature of the process of psychotherapy itself. Therapy entails not only non-reciprocal intimacy, but *non-reciprocal gratification* as well. The patient on the one hand is reminded at appropriate times (e. g., phases of resistance) that progress in therapy is essentially a non-quantifiable, long-term process subject to fluctuations and, especially, regressions and is accordingly warned not to judge its success by how gratifying any one session or series of sessions happens to feel. Furthermore, he may even be told that he can expect periods of time in which he will feel more frustrated than satisfied. The therapist, on the other hand—apart from the higher, non-materialistic satisfactions that are supposed to come from actively facilitating progress in the work at hand—expects to receive a remuneration for each week's services that cannot waver and is to be delivered in the most quantifiable form conceivable: money. The contractual obligation to pay and, particularly, the amount that is paid is therefore dependent not on the qualitative level of performance (which even in the best of therapists is quite variable) and most definitively not upon the patient's perception of the benefits that have been received. In addition, it is generally understood that if the therapist is deprived of his expected monetary gratification for more than a very short time, that therapy *must* discontinue. Thus, the therapist may enjoy the ebb and flow and long-term meaningfulness of the unpredictable progress of the therapeutic couple, but unlike the patient he must also be regularly paid for his participation. I am aware that the therapeutic rationale for such a gross non-reciprocity of gratification is that it realistically reflects and is the consequence of an equally gross non-reciprocity when it comes to the division of labor: the patient comes to the therapeutic hour and does not work at all to enhance the quality of the therapist's life (often, in fact, strives to devalue it), but struggles only to help himself, while the therapist, forbidding himself the use of his time and energy to attend to his own issues, focuses instead exclusively on those of the patient, and in order to redress this outstanding inequity of psychic investment he expects to be paid.

While this sounds plausible on one level—the economic one—it introduces on another level a double bind into therapy, certainly at least from the standpoint of the patient, who in no way regards what is transpiring interpersonally as an economic transaction (I have written about this and other double binds in psychotherapy elsewhere [Alper 1992].) Can this be resolved? One way, perhaps, is to understand that the greatest contaminant to therapy is not transferential, but economic: it is basically packaged and presented as a service for a fee, which, of course, commercializes it. So if psychotherapy really is an art, as I believe, then the same thing happens to it when it is professionalized and commercialized as happens to art when it is commercialized: it sooner or later sinks to a level of lowest common denominator so as to be marketed en masse. In the case when the product is the art of psychotherapy, it means that therapy is likely to be conceptualized as a technological artifact so as to be amenable to marketing. It follows that the chief mental health product for the consumer will be, of course, the most efficient technique. And the antidote to this downward commercial pull, the only antidote I know, is a profound, non-materialistic, generative love for the work itself (not unlike that of the true artist) that, while recognizing the considerable value in today's society of money and prestige, will see it at best as a distant secondary gain.

For someone, therefore, who wishes to radically withdraw from an intimate engagement, without having to face any of the consequences (as, for example, the previously mentioned patient's boyfriend did) then a tempting way out—continually reinforced by our opportunistic, high-tech culture—is to try to put a price tag on and to quantify what is essentially psychic and meaningful. To act, however, as though the main value of an interpersonal transaction is economic is to ignore the fact that money—except when it rightly supersedes all other concerns because it represents the only feasible means of meeting the security needs in a legitimate existential crisis, such as, for example, involving one's health—is only important if the worth of what it is being used for is commensurately materialistic: if one is purchasing a product designed to satisfy a basically utilitarian function. If the money, however, is for a service of purportedly profound human meaning, such as psychotherapy, then it must be measured according to appropriately non-materialistic values.

It is obvious that this is significantly harder to do than it sounds, if only because our society has increasingly insisted on putting a price tag on everything, including human services (psychotherapy, medicine), injuries to the mind and body (to be determined by malpractice suits), and so-called gifts of love (to be expressed in the economic exchange known as presents). Since the fine line between materialistic and humanistic values, which everyone knows exists somewhere, has been inextricably blurred by our technological culture, it has become that much easier if one wishes—when confronted with an implicit or explicit demand to act out of a personal center in accordance with the needs of the self—to step over onto the economic side of the line, protesting, in so many words, "I can't afford that," and thereby to safely withdraw from an interpersonal situation that may have nothing to do with money. We have all been witness to endless variations of this scenario: "I can't afford to: be in a relation-

ship now; get married now; have a child now; get divorced; go
to therapy; change careers."

To the other, who believed he or she was involved in something far more meaningful than profit or loss, who is now faced
with a radical withdrawal from what was perceived as an existential engagement, it cannot help but feel like a demoraliz-
ing and senseless abandonment. And it can be almost too painful to bear, to be forced to realize that someone has suddenly
turned their back on what was thought to be a mutually intimate bond, and has not only retreated into an espousal of
frankly narcissistic values but has begun to retrospectively insist
(as was the case with my patient's boyfriend) that no other issue
has ever been at stake. As such, it is an obvious although telling example of being intimacy-blind.

FORGETTING A SELF

The patient, a young, attractive, intelligent, sensitive woman
who approaches each foray onto the singles scene with a kind
of poignant hopefulness that she may be on the verge of finding what she is looking for, is once again crestfallen. She met
a man, she tells me, who is "charming, handsome, sexy, narcissistic, and elusive—you know, just the kind I like [giggles],"
and who seems as drawn to her as she to him. During the hour
that they speak excitedly to one another he touches on any
number of vital aspects of his recent and past life: his parents'
divorce when he was thirteen; his teenage marriage; his wife
leaving him while he was still an undergraduate; his passionate ambition to turn his life around and make a success of
himself; his subsequent precocious rise to the prestigious position of new products development manager of a major manu-
facturer of computer software; the wonderful house he personally designed and had built in upstate New York; the deeply

satisfying, dream-come-true, sumptuous catered parties he was thereafter able to triumphantly host within the confines of his very own, castle-like home. And at the end of this breathless, rags-to-riches self-narrative—as though to graciously make sure he would never overlook the presence of the woman who seemed so enraptured at what he was saying—he smilingly inquired, "By the way, have you ever attended one of the parties at my house?"

The effect on my patient is eerie. Spookily, in a flash, what seemed a budding person-to-person intimacy is obliterated and she feels reduced to a tabula rasa. Is it possible, she wonders, if her presentation of self is so vapid that it can be literally misperceived? Can she spend an entire hour, ardently expressing herself, immersing herself in the other, only to be totally unrecognized?

Unfortunately, in the microcosm of the singles scene, such failure to even existentially recognize the other is commonplace: a woman who has slept with a man several times a year ago unexpectedly encounters him in a different venue and with a genuinely puzzled look, shyly asks, "Do I know you?" The impact can then be uncanny, as it was with my patient, as though parts of the self had inexplicably been whited-out.

What this shows, in dramatic form, is the incredible difference between consensual validation when it comes to perception of the outside world, where everyone is obligated to agree if they wish to be considered sane, and the freedom each of us has to willfully distort the inner world and especially the true self of the other at any time and for any purpose.

When that occurs, the result is immediate, defensive confusion. Nothing can undermine the confidence of a person more quickly than the realization that her presence did not register at all. The first question then is who is responsible for the oversight: the person for failing to sufficiently articulate her presence so as to make it at least memorable enough to be remembered; or the other who has perhaps demonstrated a peculiar incapacity to take in what is authentically and humanly there?

Only human beings, it seems, have the luxury of being misperceived on this psychic level. Other species, ethologists tell us— thanks to the automatic operation of fixed action patterns, key stimuli acting as releasers for innate releasing mechanisms (IRMs)—are guaranteed species recognition. But what are the key stimuli emanating from the true self that elicit recognition? A crucial distinction, which everyone senses, is that no matter how potent such key stimuli may be, the other has no compulsion whatsoever to respond: there is no ethological program, as there is in lower animals, that compels a fixed-action pattern of recognition-response. The lone exception in human beings, according to Lorenz (1982), may be certain IRMs in infants such as the bulging forehead, fatty cheeks, and "the shaky, sweet walk" (p. 164) that trigger the parental care response.

By contrast, when it comes to adult–adult recognition among people, there is obviously considerable latitude, so much so that the simple acknowledgment of existential aspects of the self of the other is subject to the person's defensive needs of the moment. This becomes glaringly apparent when someone knows another, but just barely, and uses that to transform him into a total stranger.

It might be time now to try to answer the question: What are the key stimuli emanating from the other that signal that a person's true self has been recognized? While, of course, there are wide variations, a critical common denominator, I believe, is that the person perceives that the other is in attunement with what she herself considers the core characteristics of the self, which first of all includes the fundamental intimacy needs. When this is so, the other characteristically manifests not only knowledge but respect for the individual's self, and such respect is shown in a sensitive awareness of the appropriate interpersonal boundaries. When these conditions are met, it can be said that the person has acquired *significance* in the eyes of the other. Such significance is displayed by the other especially when he comes into closer contact with central aspects of the self. Furthermore, if the other wishes to go beyond mere recognition, and to respond more intimately, nurturance, patience, empathy, and investment of time are brought to bear. All can be viewed as key stimuli emanating from the other which reveal that perception of the person's true self has been psychically registered. It follows that the corollary is that the absence of such key stimuli is an equally conclusive sign that no such recognition has taken place.

If we return to our initial question—what are the key stimuli emanating from a person which indicates the *presence* of a true self—I think we can say in general they will include: the good faith investment of the self into whatever it is doing (the antithesis, that is, of the famous Sartrean bad faith); and the expression, elaboration, and articulation of the true self as opposed to the compulsion to hide it (with a false self). It is for this reason that when someone feels that her self has been sufficiently present in whatever she is interpersonally enacting so as to merit recognition (as my patient certainly did), but somehow doesn't get it, she typically sustains the profound narcissistic injury of being existentially misperceived.

It is therefore easy to understand that the capacity of people to intentionally white out the existential presence of the self of the other has considerable power to control, given its almost irresistible toxic impact. Many years ago, Spitz (1965) in classic studies on hospitalization showed the lethal effect that the complete lack of human touch could have on the newborn infant. Subsequently, influenced by Lorenz, he began to explore the possible ethological basis for the exchange of signals that can be observed soon after birth between the mother and her infant. Spitz found that between 3 and 6 months of age a smiling response in the infant could be elicited by certain characteristic signs of an adult face. According to Spitz, the key stimuli acting as releasers eliciting the infant's smiling response were the eyes and the mouth. Interestingly enough, these key stimuli did not have to belong to a human face and worked as well with an inanimate Halloween mask donned by an experimenter, provided that the necessary spatial configuration was simulated by the mask. Spitz therefore concluded that the infant who smiles at a face at 3 months does not really recognize an individual face, but is reacting in a programmed, ethological, almost mechanical fashion. Indeed, it would be another 4 to 6 months before the infant could legitimately be said to be able to identify and recognize an individual human face, most famously shown by the infant who reacts with anxiety or cries when a stranger other than the mother draws near.

It is obvious that no such instinct is detectable in grownups, who enjoy incomparably greater flexibility and control over the residue of their infant "stranger response" to the extent that they can almost effortlessly simulate it. In other words, any of us can at will perversely transmute any key aspect of another's self into something strange and unrecognizable. The effect of that is a little like pouring out our hearts on an issue that is dear to us only to be greeted with, "What do you mean?" When that occurs, and it happens in one form or another all too frequently, we are stopped dead in our tracks; we must go back, regroup, and start from zero. The greatest of all reductions, however, is to go from a self to a stranger. We are then placed in the position of asking ourselves, "What kind of a self would I need to be in order for my existence to make an impression (since my true self appears invisible)?" It is a question that cannot meaningfully be answered and it would be foolish to even try—one more example of the pernicious efficacy of the strategy of being intimacy-blind.

TO DOUBLE BIND

Gregory Bateson (1956), the architect of the theory of the double bind, defined it as an insidiously untenable position in which an individual is caught in the crossfire of contradictory, mixed-level messages, each of which carries a heavy penalty for being disobeyed or ignored, and simultaneously prevented not only from trying to extricate himself or herself from the very same untenable position but even from talking about it. Subsequently, the plight of the double-bind victim has passed into mainstream consciousness in the guise of the familiar no-win situation, being "damned if you do and damned if you don't." Originally, however, the double bind was considered the province of the mental health professional; Bateson himself believed that he had seen evidence that so-called schizogenic mothers, by repeatedly and unconsciously double-binding their hapless offspring, could actually engender the disease called schizophrenia. If that were the case, perhaps the process could be arrested, or even reversed. Ambitious, strategic-minded therapists such as Jay Haley (1958) began to wonder if they could somehow turn the double bind to their own use, thus giving birth to the technique of paradoxical injunction, of double-binding the patient for his or her own good, so to speak. In the next chapter I discuss, from my own point of view, the fate of the double bind in contemporary psychotherapy, especially as it pertains to patients on the singles scene who, more often than not, are preoccupied with issues of control.

Here, however, I want to emphasize the universality of the double bind, the fact that it appears in various forms in many facets of modern life. In the opening chapter, under the heading "Presumed Innocent," I alluded to the obvious and dramatic example of the O. J. Simpson jury being sequestered. On the one hand, they were instructed to render the most difficult, existential decision possible, to assume the god-like role of being a judge of the life, death, and future of another human being, and on the other hand they were treated like puppets or children—told what room to go to, when to get up, when to go to sleep, what to read, what not to read, when to make love and when not to. And, of course, they were forbidden to think, let alone discuss, that such a thing as a double bind exists.

In the more mundane interpersonal world of the singles scene, patients do not generally, of course, complain of such protracted, horrific double binds as Simpson trial jurors had to live with every day of their sequestration. Nor do they even explicitly speak, except on rare occasions, in terms of the double bind. But they do give off numerous signs that they are troubled by a vague, or not so vague, feeling of being persistently controlled by someone or some force, of being confused as to why they are in the untenable position they seem to be in, and of being resentful that they are so unsuccessful at extricating themselves. This is not so surprising when you think about it. All of the strategies of control that I have delineated—the fascist emotion, narcissistic giving, being intimacy-blind, addictive relating, behavioral puppetry—have in common that they paint the other into a corner, whereupon they punish him if he stays, punish him if he tries to leave, and punish him if he endeavors to raise to consciousness the subject of his mistreatments.

If these, then, are the elements of the double bind, and they are, how does it characteristically manage to control? First of all, through mystification. The person trapped in an untenable interpersonal situation that he cannot overcome, cannot escape from and, perhaps most poignantly, cannot name is puzzled in a rather hopeless way. Far from the generative musing of a self that is on the brink of launching itself into a Winnicottian adventure of creative living (as so evocatively described by Bollas 1992), this is a rather desolate interrogation. The double bind, because of its nature, cannot facilitate development or process and is accordingly experienced as profoundly uncreative, which is the point because in so doing it keeps the person in his place. Trust is therefore eroded and the unavoidable conclusion that there is no future in relating within the context of a double bind leads to interpersonal despair. It follows that whatever prospects there were for intimacy are nullified and distance is ensured.

Someone who manages to put another into a double bind converts interrelating into strategic gameplaying and is now in the one-up position of being able to watch the person try to squirm free. From an intersubjective standpoint, a double binding transaction is subversively reductive: by maneuvering the other into a deceptively frustrating trap, his attention cannot help but begin to fixate on the immediate dilemma. Nothing makes more sense to the person upon whom a double bind has been imposed than to channel his energies toward a plan of escape. Its impact is analogous to that of any other unambiguously adverse situation. Such common sense, self-evident reallocation of interest, however, effectively camouflages the fact that the relationship has abruptly and qualitatively changed from one where there was at least a chance for intimacy to one where the only real issues are who is going to control and who is going to be controlled. As a strategy of control, because of its almost exclusive focus on manipulation and gamesmanship, it is an example of behavioral puppetry.

THE ENFORCER

In discussing the strategy of the fascist emotion, I tried to describe some of the key elements of control inherent in ordinary impulsive anger with the intent to harm. Now I would like to point to the behavioral interaction that perhaps best encapsulates such a strategy of control: that of intimidation, which might be defined as the tactic of using the natural power of anger to control as a tool to narcissistically manipulate the behavior of the other.

There is a difference, of course, between being angry and being intimidating. An act of anger is characteristically short-term, impulsive, reactive, and non-strategic, and to the degree that it is often spontaneous and unplanned, more honest. An act of intimidation is considerably more calculated, long-term, and strategic. The anger that is almost always at its core is therefore comparatively muted.

Intimidation works in several ways.

1) By reminding the other what is in store if he crosses the line or incurs the intimidator's anger.

2) By displaying conspicuous and aggressive vigilance. Someone who is willing to invest the necessary energy that goes into advertising that one is steadily monitoring the behavior of the other for any transgressions is intimidating. On an interactional, psychical, and dynamic level, intimidation is modeled on the actions of the policeman. Like the policeman, the interpersonal intimidator assumes a militant stance, restlessly patrols the designated boundaries of his territory, and shows a readiness to enforce submission to authority and to punish offenders.

3) In the same sense that a policeman is intimidating because it is understood he carries weapons, and has training in how to use them and authority to implement his aggressive intentions, someone who is intimidating likewise must be perceived as an individual who is definitely not a toothless tiger, who can make good on threats.

It follows that such a person will be viewed circumspectly as someone who has either been challenged or provoked in the past and has viciously retaliated or who has so far been so convincingly menacing that he has never had to prove himself. And the fact that the intimidator typically does not back away from the punitive aspects of anger is in itself intimidating, creating the aura, in the psychological interpersonal sense, of an enforcer—an individual who makes his way by brute force. In other words, the realization that the intimidator has seemingly chosen a style of relating that is based on constant pressuring of the other, and does not appear to be uncomfortable with the obvious anxiety his persona evokes but perhaps even relishes it, is most unnerving. The impression is that this person—who, must have unimaginably more aggressive energy at his disposal than the ordinary person if he can maintain such a high level of belligerence—is at bottom a warrior (although a mean-spirited one) and therefore to be feared.

By contrast, ordinary impulsive anger with the intent to harm, while thoroughly unpleasant and anxiety-arousing, seems more human. Both aim to teach a punitive lesson, but intimidation seems to punish for punishment's sake and to use punishment as an interpersonal modus operandi. Perhaps most disturbing of all is that both elicit fear of humiliation, which may be defined as the traumatizing shame one feels whenever one perceives oneself, or believes others perceive one, as being helpless to prevent or remedy specific acts directed toward one that are clearly intended to degrade one's dignity. The fear of humiliation is understandably stronger when it involves someone who is viewed as intimidating. On the other hand, there is always a certain fear of the shame that can arise if taken unawares by an outburst of anger, one is revealed as embarrassingly unable to protect oneself, to fight back if necessary, or in the worst-case scenario is exposed as a person who responds to the slightest attack by retreating in a cowardly fashion. A substantial part of the almost universal fear of being surprised by someone else's anger—conferring upon it its considerable power to control the behavior of the other and of oneself in those instances where unprocessed defensive anger threatens to turn against the self—is the dread that shame will be the aftermath of the angry eruption. Such fear is compounded in the case of the individual regarded as an enforcer, who is more than likely to seize upon the capacity of anger to produce shame as a handy interpersonal whip to keep the other in line.

Patients who elect to go into therapy, or who are driven to do so because of narcissistic injuries sustained on the singles scene, are often preoccupied with questions as to whether they are in control, being controlled, or too controlling. Not surprisingly, in the course of therapy such questions become thematic and in the next chapter I examine their impact from the standpoint of the patient and from the standpoint of the therapist.

4

Therapy

THE PSYCHOTHERAPIST:
AS TRUE AND FALSE SELF

Although it may be years (if at all) before patients become
genuinely interested in exploring the subtler dimensions of
their true and false selves, almost from the first moment they
set eyes on their therapist, they want to know what he or she
is really like.

In his seminal paper, "Ego Distortion in Terms of True and
False Self" (1960), Winnicott likens the true self to the "spontaneous gesture" (beginning in infancy with the tending of the
good enough mother) and regards it as the root of all subsequent healthy and creative living. By contrast, he says of the
false self, "The False Self has one positive and very important
function . . . to hide the True Self, which it does by compliance with environmental demands" (p. 147). Winnicott con-
cludes with the crucial statement, "*Whereas the True Self feels
real, the existence of a False Self results in a feeling unreal or a
sense of futility*" (p. 148).

It is to be remembered, of course, that the true and the false
self that Winnicott and analysts who follow him are speaking

about refer almost exclusively to the patient. But if we are considering the perspective of the patient—in his quest to puzzle out the real identity of his therapist—what is it that he is likely to encounter?

The therapist the patient meets is embedded in the therapeutic situation. And because of its structured, artificial setup, its precise rules of behavior and well-defined frame, this therapeutic situation will necessarily lack the fluid, spontaneous, open-ended creativity that any other non-rule-governed, dynamic, whole, human relationship can have. It is from this standpoint that the therapeutic relationship that is derivative of it can perhaps never be experienced as a whole relationship, but always as only part or piece of a human bond, and therefore *does not feel real—it feels false*.

It follows that there may be an area of transference analysis that has been neglected. Transference may not be just the outcome of regressive illness or reaction to objects (internal or external). It may in addition be a normal (as well as transferential) outcome: an attempt at reparation to make a relationship (within and to the therapeutic situation) that does not feel whole or real into one more integrated and authentic. If this is so, patients may not only be projecting derivatives of their intrapsychic sense of conflict and fragmentation. They may also be projecting a sense of interpersonal fragmentation peculiar to the therapeutic situation that is *real* and not transferentially distorted. These splits that patients are struggling to resist, defend themselves against, or heal *may also include splits in the therapeutic relationship*.

Yet, perhaps because it can be a narcissistic injury to their personal humanism, therapists tend to deny or minimize the pain that is caused by the therapeutic relationship itself and see it instead as intrapsychic resistance. Unlike physicians, who can reasonably attempt to quantitatively justify the pain contained in their treatment through a cost-versus-benefits analysis, therapists can never be sure the pain they are causing will ever be justified. If this is so, there may be a concept of the *real resistance* (as in real relationship versus transferential relationship), wherein it is understood that there is a certain and necessary artificiality, restrictedness, and unreality implicit in the therapeutic situation that the patient will eventually perceive, and appropriately, resist. In this sense, at least some of what is usually called the patient's resistance is an attempt either to defend himself or to break through the false and unreal-seeming therapeutic situation per se in an effort to find and talk to the suspected hidden true self of the therapist.

Although there will be as many false techniques as there are false therapeutic selves, a common one will center on the belief in a code of conduct for the therapist so protected that it is held to be almost universally true. And what therefore we might call a *false-self technique* will emerge whenever there is a concerted attempt to somehow quantify the interaction of a designated principle of behavior with a live clinical situation. Such false-self techniques arise when there is the conviction that behavior can be predicted, that there is a correct, sanitized code of behavior that can be projected into the future—like a predictive hypothesis—and experimentally confirmed or falsified in the clinical here-and-now. By contrast, what might be termed a *true-self technique* does not *precede* treatment, but imaginatively evolves and is validated in the course of treatment. Finally, the most commonly used defense (because it is easiest) of the false self of the therapist is the employment of a sterile, false technique: even more than neutrality, it can provide a defensive haven for countertransferences, especially false-self countertransferences in which the therapist is heavily invested in being or appearing radically other than he or she is.

Although it is often taken for granted that therapists have, or should have, therapeutic personalities (which include warmth), the fact is many do not. This may be because someone can be their creative, spontaneous, alive, true self and still be rather nasty (if that is part of their true self). So the true self must be therapeutic and now we can immediately define what we mean by a therapeutic personality: a therapeutic personality is a true self whose presence is therapeutic.

Winnicott (1960), in his paper on the true and false self, spoke of the "good enough mother" (p. 145). We can amend this to the *good enough therapist*. The good enough therapist will recognize and admit (at some level, I believe) the problematical, existential nature of the therapeutic relationship and situation. He or she senses that there is something forever incomplete, not whole, always denying, inherently contradictory, paradoxical, and incongruent, and (to these degrees) unreal-feeling about the therapeutic situation, but also knows this does not mean that the *therapist as a person* cannot be whole. And this is what the good enough therapist does: *holds* the human deficits and paradoxical splits of the therapeutic situation and heals them as well as possible *exactly* as he holds the deficits and splits *within* the patient. In this regard, the good enough therapist realizes that the best answer to the patient's frequent charge of falseness and unreality of the therapeutic situation is not more and better technique, not simply a passing-the-buck analysis of the patient's resistances. It is an empathic, therapeutic true self of the therapist that can contain and make more whole, and therefore more bearable, the splits in the therapeutic situation.

THE DOUBLE BIND IN PSYCHOTHERAPY

In the last chapter I stressed the universality of the double bind and its relevance to the strategies of control that I have been delineating. Here, I want to focus on its often overlooked dynamic presence in the therapeutic situation.

It will be obvious that the view here differs sharply from traditional family systems double-bind theorists whose primary therapeutic strategy is to unravel a pathological metacommunicational bottleneck originating in the family. By contrast, the psychotherapeutic double bind considered here is essentially not one of paradoxical messages and conflicting levels of communication. Instead, it is one arising from *a conflict of incompatible levels of intimacy: specifically, the unspoken of conflict between technique and intimacy.*

For the patient, the central double bind is that he or she is put into the role of *non-reciprocal intimacy with a professional stranger.* The central double bind, as far as the therapist is concerned, is that—in a dyadic setting evocative of profound intimacy—he or she is constrained *to behave in a manner largely dictated by an impersonal, professional technique* (regardless of how empathically that technique may be manifested).

From the perspective of the patient, he or she is asked, on the one hand, to slowly and regressively sink to the deepest level of dependency, the most basic child-like transferential love (or hate). The patient is then expected to organize himself or herself and to pay for it. Patients are thereby asked to put two things together that in our culture are essentially antithetical and almost never go well together: structured, rule-defined, fee-oriented, non-reciprocal behavior and a firm request for the most candid, intimate, sustained self-disclosure. There does not seem to be a relationship analogue in our culture to help prepare the patient for the demands of the therapeutic situation.

On the other hand, it is not only the patient who is caught up in the paradoxical effects of the psychotherapeutic double bind. As therapists, we are subject to certain ambiguities and perplexing, open-ended questions that reflect an underlying double bind. There is, for example, the question regarding professional identity: Are psychotherapists essentially objective, using their human relating as a tool to help, or are they basically caring people who instead use their objectivity as a tool to help? Indeed, the double bind inherent in the therapeutic situation may conveniently allow some therapists to switch—according to their countertransferential needs—from being intimate, caring and empathic, to being objective and ever-vigilant of the frame.

Now, to what extent do therapists deal with what might be called the double standard of truthfulness implied in the therapeutic situation? After all, therapists generally use two distinct languages: one for patients, highly censored and constructed in accordance with the protocols of technique; the other with colleagues, out of earshot of patients, franker, freer, and less censored. This can create a discrepancy for patients, who are usually encouraged to use the language of maximum self-disclosure.

And how do therapists sort out the professional need to evaluate time as money from the corresponding patient need for the therapist to be fully and humanly present in the here and now, and, therefore, to a certain extent, to be empathically *blinded* to time? There is, of course, no simple answer to this.

Psychotherapists who are unclear on this issue may experience the shadow of the clock hovering over the session like a meter running. The allusion to therapists that is sometimes heard as almost prostitutes of relating—"You're the only one who listens to me, but I'm paying you"—may not come just from patient hostility. This difficulty is partly rooted in the fact that there is no analogue in our culture for selling our relating. The artist who has to set a price tag on his art may be the closest we can come. Yet the artist can rely upon a somewhat natural temporal division between the process of his art and the subsequent marketing of his art, and use that to separate them.

It follows that the double bind is much greater for therapists, who are unable to take refuge in any such clean division much as they and their patients might try their best to isolate the economics of therapy from the process and purpose of therapy. In fact, by contrast, therapists work by the hour, charge by the hour, and can easily be perceived as doing a kind of humane piecework. There is a sense, economically speaking, that therapists are ruled by the clock. This sobering truth, if it needs any reinforcement, is reflected in their income tax form. They do estimated taxes and are listed as self-employed businessmen and businesswomen.

Is it not logical, therefore, to ask what is their business? If psychotherapy is their business, what is their product? Are therapists delivering the product they deliver (whatever that is) because it is the best product they can produce in their economic pursuit of profit? Or is it the other way around? Are therapists really unmaterialistic (which is not to say they do not appreciate and enjoy the benefits of being financially comfortable)? Are they, instead, just realists who have made a decision to try to earn a living doing the thing they most love, and therefore accept that there is an unavoidable business aspect to what they do? Few therapists are sufficiently clear on this point, but then the culture as a whole is not clear about it either. And, finally, there is another confusing question: What percentage of their interest in a given session is interest in the patient, and what percentage of their interest is interest in earning the fee for the session?

The psychotherapeutic situation begins with the delimiting of a whole, normal, dynamic, human relationship, and it does this in order to dispel interfering variables so as to focus heightened attention on intrapsychic and interpersonal disturbances. Because of this initial delimiting, it may well be that whatever subsequent growth occurs is at least partially caused by this. However, ironically, here is where the double bind comes in: the patient does not know this, even if he knows it intellectually. Instead, what he basically experiences for a long time is the delimiting of the interpersonal setting. It is a delimiting that takes the special form of juxtaposing human relationship variables (professional technique and intimacy) that experientially do not belong together and therefore put him into a double bind that both puzzles and erodes his sense of interpersonal reality. Historically, therapists have tended to focus on the payoff of this human experiment, and to use it to justify the ongoing double bind that is one price tag, among others, for their patients' progress.

Finally, my view differs from traditional double bind theorists (Jackson 1963) who see transference as a kind of externally, manipulatively induced form of childishness. In spite of this, it is useful to look at transference from the standpoint of the double-bind theorists as not just the outcome of regressive illness or projective reaction to objects (internal or external). From the standpoint of the double bind, then, the therapeutic situation is not a tenable position. This means that once a patient is put into it, forces within will immediately conspire to get him out of it, in spite of any countering positive transference or therapeutic alliance. This is because psychoanalytic psychotherapy, in just one of its revolutionary side effects, joins two strange bedfellows: technique and intimacy. Since they never have gotten along well together, it was inevitable there would be immediate affects and effects, forcing a necessary emotional clash and dialogue.

If one wishes to understand the connection between the double bind and transference, it is revealing to look at what transference accomplishes. From the standpoint of the double bind, transference does a lot. Transference takes a professional relationship and transforms it into an intensely intimate relationship. Transference takes two strangers who have only just met and transforms them into lifelong blood relatives. It takes two incompatible levels of intimacy and makes them complementary and reciprocal, even if negatively so. It can thereby still the anxiety that one is intimately opening up before a professional stranger who may turn out to be cold-blooded, vengeful, critical, indifferent, or only interested in using the patient for monetary profit. It does this; it rescues the patient by pulling out from the terrifying void of professional estrangement something even more magically familiar than a trusted friend—a parent or sibling. Seen in this light, transference accomplishes a great deal. Because so much attention has been paid to its infantile roots, its skillfulness has probably not been given sufficient credit. Yet, looked at strictly and only from the vantage point of the double bind, we can sum it up by saying that transference (apart from everything else attributed to it) is also restitution and denial. It is a magical attempt to resolve the double bind of non-reciprocal intimacy by substituting for the actual psychotherapeutic relationship an early parent/ sibling-child imago which is far more reassuringly representative of reciprocal intimacy (and this is so even if the transference is negative).

It should be obvious that the area of the double bind in psychotherapy is an intrinsically structurally ambivalent space that can serve as an unconscious projective screen for the corresponding ambivalent feelings of the participants: for the therapist who may be occasionally unsure of his stance vis-à-vis the paradoxical nature of his role (as I believe is true, to a greater or lesser extent, of all of us) and for the patient who comes to us from the singles scene who, more often than not, is preoccupied if not tormented with issues of control.

CONTROL GAMES IN THERAPY

The patient who can no longer stand the pain of being on the singles scene and comes to therapy will understandably arrive in a state of deprivation. Feeling cheated, he may have masochistically low or narcissistically, grandiosely great expectations. Such a patient may want to be nursed back to health slowly and safely, immediately gratified, masterfully taken charge of, entertained along the way, educated in how to become a winner, or comforted for being a loser in the game of love, and so on. At bottom, the person will be rather hopeless and unable to believe in the possibility of establishing a trusting relationship with anyone, least of all with a professional stranger. More likely there will be thoughts of how to manipulate the therapy so as to get what he thinks he wants, what to expect, what to demand, what to disclose, what to hold back and so on. It will be difficult not to compare the new therapeutic encounter with the current or recent relationship on the singles scene that has proved so disappointing and to speculate on what the prospects are this time for feeling the least bit good or satisfied. Typically, the patient who has felt frustrated and boxed in by the other will be hypersensitive to the terms of the therapeutic contract, specifically the therapist's personal policy regarding the requirements for makeups, notice to be given for cancellations, and payment of the fee, which will be unconsciously evaluated according to the degree of rigid control it is perceived to manifest. There will be almost immediate transference to the double-bind aspects of the psychotherapeutic situation. In order to discover just how controlling the therapist really is, the patient will try to see what lies underneath or beyond the protective technique, what part of it is reflective of a truly genuine, caring, empathic, and intimate self and what part is the strategic embodiment of a comparatively self-interested, scheming, and indifferent person.

Does this sound familiar? Not surprisingly, soon after the patient enters therapy, there will be a transferential enactment of the game we have alluded to as "getting real," and he will examine the therapist for signs of what he or she really feels. The double-bind aspects of the therapeutic situation create a natural dynamic tension which drives this game: on the one hand, the patient is meeting an artificial therapeutic person, the likes of which he has hardly encountered in the outside real world, who may almost never, in his presence, raise his or her voice, get sick, go to the bathroom, eat food, become visibly upset, angry, confused, sad, or openly vulnerable, seem concerned with personal problems, act egocentrically, or appear uninterested or bored, and, on the other hand, there is everyone else the patient has met on the singles scene who behaves more or less in the opposite fashion. It is inevitable that there will be some intrapsychic or interpersonal effort to penetrate the curtain of the professional persona and to flush the therapist out. From this suspicious state of mind, what will be considered real in the therapist are secret thoughts that reveal what the therapist actually thinks of the patient: telltale moments of anger, irritation, loss of control, mistakes, apparent chinks in the code of professional conduct, flashes of atypical behavior, and so on. From the standpoint of countertransference, the therapist must contend with recurrent feelings of insecurity concerning how uncomfortable he or she is with the required interpersonal artificiality of the role versus the nagging recognition that it is likely to be impossible to ever responsibly satisfy the patient's demand to be real. Indeed, to gratify the patient with revelations of the real in the way patients usually want is to offer a compliant false self. By contrast, the task of the therapist is to integrate the abstractness and social unreality necessitated by the therapeutic stance with his or her true self in a manner that is both meaningful and non-compromising: that is, neither to lose oneself in a self-eradicating neutrality nor to overcompensate with unwarranted displays of what I have termed the pseudo-real (in the fashion, perhaps, of some well-meaning but overly zealous gestalt therapists). Inasmuch as double-bind issues cannot ever be fully resolved, the therapeutic stance will always represent a delicate mixture of the therapist's true and false selves. Accordingly, the therapist recognizes that the constraints of the role, especially the pressure to be neutral, will act as a constant filter between what is interpersonally experienced and the freedom to immediately react to what the patient says and does in a natural, real, here-and-now way.

For their part, patients will be unduly suspicious, confused, sometimes paranoid vis-à-vis their initial contact with the double-bind aspects of the therapeutic situation. It can be forgotten that technique is as difficult for patients to learn as it is for therapists. The technique they have to learn, however, is not the technique of treatment issues. They have to learn that this strange silence is not meanness or withholding; that this maddening neutrality is not deadness nor hollowness; that this person who volunteers almost nothing personal about himself or herself is not hiding or afraid. In short, they must come to understand that technique is an aspect of a person, to relate to technique that way, and to trust it, if they can. They have to learn that the technique they first meet embedded in a person is somehow part of a long, therapeutic process, and part of a whole therapeutic person, that perhaps may benefit them.

It is too much, of course, to expect that patients can do this in the beginning; more likely they will regard their brush with technique as being, at bottom, a professional variant of narcissistic giving: they will wonder for whose benefit does technique as such exist. Understandably, they will want to test the extent to which their therapist's particular policies—regarding the need for makeups, the amount of notice required to be given for cancellations, the terms of payment—reflect his or her real self. Patients will sense that their therapist's policies on these matters may touch directly on the narcissistic needs that underlie their professional role-playing. By challenging or resisting the therapeutic contract that is offered to them—"What's the reason for that?" . . . "I know other people whose therapist doesn't require makeups"—patients may hope to create cracks in the therapist's composure through which they can observe the depth of his need to get paid, to be in control of the time frame of the session, and to superintend the progression of the therapy.

Although countertransferential phenomena are often described in the literature (when not considered effects of the patient's projective identification) as pertaining to the therapist, it is worth noting—from the standpoint of control games—the *countertransference traps* that are often unconsciously set by patients in order to flush out the real in their therapist. A countertransference trap arises when there is a transferential enactment by the patient of a control game that is designed to engender a specific response in the therapist. Inasmuch as there is little intent to communicate unconsciously, a countertransference trap will differ from projective identification and force, rather than the power of expressiveness, will be relied upon. Calling into question the therapist's policy, knowing this is likely to be an area of personal vulnerability, is one way to apply force. Another is to convert the privilege which every patient is granted—to articulate negative transference with impunity—into an opportunity for rejecting and abusing the therapist and thereby playing a therapeutic variant of the game alluded to as "Like it is." It is a well-kept secret that psychotherapists, just like other people, do not like to be mistreated. Indeed, perhaps because they are typically more sensitive than the average person, they like it less. But the catch-22 is that they are professionally trained not only to bite the bullet, but to encourage their patients to air their hostilities freely, a decided disadvantage patients often cannot resist exploiting. What follows are clinical vignettes, culled from my practice, that illustrate some of the ways patients will transferentially enact control games in order to lure the therapist into compromising his or her therapeutic stance.

EXAMPLES OF COUNTERTRANSFERENCE TRAPS

I am a novice therapist much under the influence of an admired supervisor who considers the expression of negative transference by the patient—regardless of how successfully it may sabotage my budding professionalism—as a promising sign of progress in the therapy. Accordingly, upon sensing that a patient, Mark, is having deep reservations as to whether I am the right therapist for him, I invite him to tell me candidly what he thinks of me without fear of reprisal. After some anxious moments in which he appears to be wrestling with whether he can trust me enough to speak his mind, the patient, who has often complained of his profound insecurity when it comes to meeting women, says, "You know I'm looking for help with women and . . . let's face it . . . you don't exactly strike me like you're a winner when it comes to the ladies!" This response is so out-of-the-blue, so far from what I had expected yet uncannily coming on the heels of a divorce that is producing in me typical feelings of deep abandonment that I am momentarily but unavoidably crestfallen. Nevertheless, I rally myself. Weakly I mumble, "That's okay, go on," and apparently sufficiently reassure the patient who, now grinning openly at the prospect of simultaneously getting at me while appearing to be a good patient, is happy to oblige: "Go on? You must be a masochist! Well, for one thing, I don't like the way you look . . . and (glancing pointedly at my stomach) you're kind of pudgy, too."

Prior to a session I inadvertently knock a clock that regularly stands on a bookcase shelf to the ground. When I restore it to its former position I don't notice that the small hour hand is no longer working properly, but my next patient, Sophie, a highly anxious, defensively aggressive woman who prides herself on her ability to confront people who are trying to put something over on her, does. After pointing out to me the incorrectness of the time shown by the clock, she pauses and with an embarrassed but knowing smile, asks, "I was wondering if that was some kind of therapeutic test, to see if I would notice that the clock wasn't working?"

Apart from a certain characteristic paranoid suspiciousness regarding the motives of others, this challenging inquiry suggests to me that if patients are in the habit of setting countertransference traps, as I believe, they are also susceptible to concluding, as a result of projection, that their therapists are similarly setting transference traps for them, and, secondly, in spite of the fact that the point of a control game is to subvert the autonomy of the other, patients depend on their therapists to demonstrate the professional self-discipline without which they do not think they can be helped. Patients only want their therapists to be unsettled and out of control on their own terms, and I have sometimes been amazed how at times when I feel uncertain as to what to do or even lost, patients will bend over backwards to *cover* for me, that is, to invent scenarios—such as my patient's suspicion that my broken clock was only a pretext to investigate her capacity for reality testing—meant to restore my mastery of the therapeutic situation. Finally, a further confirmation that patients only want doses of the real therapist on their own terms is the fact that whenever they accidentally bump into the therapist outside of the safety of the office, they invariably (and this has been my consistent personal experience) seem to initially regret it, in spite of the opportunity it obviously affords for subsequent voyeuristic titillation.

At the time of the incident I am about to describe, I had been in private practice over ten years and up until then, other than me and my patients, no other living creature had been visibly present in the sessions. But on this occasion the patient, Louis, a somber, inhibited man who is obsessed with doing things and having things be the way they should, completely disarms me by quietly pointing his finger in the direction of the foot of the armchair in which I am sitting and announcing, "I think that's a roach." Immediately rising from my chair I confirm his observation, much to my chagrin and, without pausing to think—acting much more like a New Yorker than a therapist—I settle the matter by stepping on it.

The awkward silence that follows, during which I uneasily ruminate as to whether I have acted professionally or not, is punctuated by my patient who, with a small, uncharacteristically mocking smile, comments, "You moved pretty quick there."

For years he has seen me as self-contained, patient, and even-humored. It had not occurred to me until that moment that his mental image of me as unhurried had also included my bodily movements, and that the sudden glimpse of me moving spontaneously, nervously, and perhaps irritably had struck him with the force of a revelation. Taken unawares, my untypical countertransferential response suggested to him that secretly I was as repelled by roaches as he was and his mocking smile seemed to say that for this moment at least, we were equals.

The patient, Florence, is an internationally known designer who is terminating therapy with me. She has finished thanking me in an obligatory fashion for some of the ways I have helped her and is now intent upon going over one last time the details of her disappointment. Just when I think I have heard it all, understood and accepted it as best I could, she sighs and glances at my feet. "And that dust underneath your armchair. It bothers me." Coming at a time when I had been hard at work to shore up my private sense of my professional competence—an important element of which is to be able to provide for patients a reasonably clean environment—the remark, short and sweet, takes me aback. Noticing this, the patient, as though consoling a desolate reminder of her former self, wearily adds,

"I'm sorry. I used to be a failure myself and to live like that. I'm just very sensitive now to the kind of image a person, especially a person who's supposed to be a professional, gives off."

Since my office is located in the East Village in Manhattan, where biking is an increasingly popular form of alternative travel, I have on occasion, when a session was scheduled to begin, opened the door of my office and been greeted by a patient *and* his bicycle. But up until Jim, a boyish, needy, athletic-looking 30-year-old man who was mystified as to why women did not consider him mature enough to be taken seriously in a relationship, I had never had a patient enter the office wearing rollerblades and proceed to skate across the carpeted floor to the couch. When this peculiar means of arriving for a session was repeated on three separate occasions, I felt compelled to address the matter in some way, although I had a hunch that no matter how sensitively I approached the issue, my patient would become defensive. I was right: when I reminded Jim of our past discussions of the child part of his personality—he had become enamored of a pop version of Eric Berne's transactional analysis wherein ego states are categorized as either parent, adult, or child—and raised the possibility that skating into my office for therapy may be an example of less than adult behavior, my patient immediately responded as if he had been parentally chided. For about fifteen minutes he launched into an impromptu, animated lecture on the brief history of rollerblading, the current popularity it was enjoying, especially in New York City, the fact that in Quebec people routinely rollerbladed each morning from their homes to their jobs. Was I aware of any of that? he innocently inquired at the conclusion of his defense. All I know, I silently and unhappily told myself, is that I am being forbidden from confronting him on what he is insisting is only an appropriate true self-expression of a child part of his personality—which meant I was to over-

look or put up with whatever track marks he was leaving in
my office carpet.

In all the years I have been in private practice as a psychotherapist, no one has ever accosted me with the unbounded
fury of Alvin, a lanky, 35-year-old student, who more or less
seemed to be in a perpetual rage that he still felt emotionally
and financially almost totally dependent on his parents' support. Up until that moment, his contempt for me had been
somewhat muted, but now it all came pouring out. Who did I
think I was, anyway—Jung? Just because I had written a book
on young artists—which he had read and which had been the
catalyst, he would later confide, for his coming to see me—did
I think I was anybody? I was nothing, a psychoanalytic nothing! He had been to a string of some of the most famous
analysts in New York and they were all nothing—they all had
essentially the same sickening spiel.

   It was the ferocity of his delivery, rather than the content,
that so dumbfounded me. He sat on the leather couch about
ten feet away, his face contorted with hatred, the words flying
out of his mouth, like verbal spit. While I did not think he was
on the brink of assaulting me, I was by no means confident he
would not. An incident popped into my mind, which Alvin had
related shortly after coming into therapy with me, concerning
his last therapist, who was a well-known analyst and author.
In just his fourth session, Alvin had proceeded to tell off his
therapist, concluding with his standard threat to terminate
therapy. "Yes, why don't you?" retorted the analyst, who proceeded to confess that he was inhibited by fears that Alvin might
at any moment hatefully attack him.

   "Alvin. . . . " I now spluttered, having no idea what to say but
fearful of appearing unduly threatened and passive. "Shut up,"
snapped Alvin. "If you say one more word, you won't get paid."

For the past two months, Alvin had neglected to turn over the money his parents dutifully sent him for therapy, and now, as I contemplated the horrifying prospect of not getting paid for two months of work in addition to taking this unbearable abuse—realizing the price I was to pay for receiving just payment was to bite my tongue and mutely accept my punishment—I felt more in the vise of my patient's control than I have ever felt.

When the session mercifully ended, when Alvin delivered his parents' check, officially terminated therapy with me, and left, violently slamming the door of my office behind him, I was forced to admit, although I did my best not to show it for at least most of that session, I hated him almost as much as he hated me. And it was a chilling, sobering experience, providing me with a powerful countertransferential insight into the corrosive nature of hate, hateful exchanges, and hateful fights—transactions that I would serenely listen to as narrated by my patients, so long as they were directed at some other.

The expression and acting out of hatred, I realized, was symbolically tantamount to ripping a person to pieces. Knowing this, people instinctively hold back from a certain level of viciously telling each other off—much as lions who fight for dominance in a pride refrain from using their killing bite, except as a last resort—and there is an understandable fear of reaching what might be called a relational point of no return. (As soon as Alvin, for example, walked out the door I knew he would never come back and that even if he did, so intense was my hostility, that I would forever be unsuitable to act as his therapist.) The spectacle of someone's hatred carries such impact that in retrospect it does not seem possible that it could have arisen as simply the dynamic product of the moment, but, instead, must have evolved. Showing hatred, therefore, is like showing that one's internal object representation of the other has for a very long time been *poisoned*. And the other cannot help but unconsciously realize and resent how hopelessly hard it will be to nurture and nurse such a sick representation of himself back into a state of health and vitality.

It follows that the release, interpersonally, of hatred controls by inducing a kind of psychic paralysis in its object. After all, how does one proceed in such a situation? On the one hand, it seems patently impossible to try to patch things up and move closer in an intimate way. On the other hand, to fight with an enemy who has declared his hatred seems clearly dangerous, while it seems almost equally dangerous to passively allow the declaration of hatred to go uncontested. There is a sense that such a person has demonstrated an alarming contempt for your fundamental need for self-esteem and therefore must be shown that if he will not control his savage aggression, you will. (The feeling of urgency that is evoked is analogous to the reaction to an obscene phone call: it is too frightening to simply allow someone to get away with that degree of harassment.)

It follows that the unchecked expression of hatred can resonate with the deepest fears one has that one is secretly despicable. There is, typically, an immediate paranoid self-doubting: "Did I somehow do something to actually warrant being openly despised?" It is rare when the initial answer to this question is a forthright "yes." Much more likely is it that there will be a countering and rallying conviction that one has been unjustly accused, bolstered by a rationalizing suspicion that the other has just gone temporarily insane.

There is an ironic twist, however, when the hateful interactions we have been describing take place in the crucible of the singles scene. If someone is intimately involved with an other who proceeds to unleash sustained hatred, there may then be a kind of paradoxical identification with the romantic aggressor. Since it is so unbearable to experience murderous rage from a love object, it can seem preferable to believe that the person is really expressing moral outrage rather than personal disgust: rather than a pathological and nightmarish transformation of love into hate, there is, perhaps, only a pathology of moral inflexibility. And armed with this desperate hope, the former love object searches his memory in order to find a plausible explanation as to why—admittedly through a tragic misunderstanding—the person may have found moral grounds for hating. It is therefore not uncommon for a patient who has been traumatized by a former lover's apparently unrelenting and heartless vilification of everything both of them cherished in the past—after recounting yet another incident of brutal derogation—to matter-of-factly and stoically conclude, "Of course, I can understand why she feels that way." Alvin was such a lover who, when he spoke about it, spent half of his time hating with all his heart the girlfriend who had recently abandoned him and half of his time moralistically defending her decision to desert him.

Deidre had cried before in therapy, but sweetly, and always in relation to the disheartening inability of some man to truly appreciate her. Until this incident, the failure to register her worth had been attributed to someone other than me. Now as I watched her body tremble with wracking sobs, and listened to her words between gasps for breath—"How could you . . . how could you *say* that?"—I realized, as never before, the full force of her accusations.

For about five minutes, alternately rocking and hugging herself, she sat on the couch and continued to sob bitterly as I searched my professional conscience to see if I could have possibly said anything monstrous enough to have produced such a tortured reaction. What I did say, as gently as I thought I could, was that Deidre—in her recurrent strident denunciations of men who in one form or another she believed had abandoned her—was perhaps unconsciously empowering a hopeless part of her self by allowing herself too readily to be overwhelmed by it.

"Do you think I actually *want* this pitiful existence of mine?" she moaned, when she finally finished crying. I was not only at a loss for words, but was aware that her dramatic display of accusatory grief had a decidedly inhibiting effect on my will-ingness in the future to be in unconscious rapport with her. Later, when I thought about this, I remembered a session in which I had commented to Deidre—upon hearing yet another account of her anguished protest to a boyfriend who was deciding to call it quits—"Well, I'll say this for you, you cer-tainly are a warrior." And she had ruefully shot back, "Yes, a masochistic warrior."

That phrase, epitomizing as it did what had just been trans-acted between Deidre and me, stayed with me. The masochist warrior, I realized, is someone who, like Deidre, must first collapse in order to fight. And when they fight, they do so pri-marily by using their past scars as weapons. They throw the ruined parts of their self in the face of their putative destroy-ers and, in effect, attack them by publicizing the evidence of their soul-murder. It is as though they cannot defend them-selves unless through retaliation and a sense of moral outrage fueled by intense feelings of victimization. To put it another way: they do not feel automatically entitled to assert their self-esteem and safeguard it from unjustified assaults *before* they are narcissistically injured. Instead, they must wait until they are wounded (and, so to speak, see their own blood). What this really means is that they can't begin a fight unless it has already been lost. From this perspective, it immediately be-comes clear that the anxiety of entering an evenly matched contest is too great for them. What they would rather do is aggressively accuse and prosecute a crime that they allege has already been perpetrated against them. What they can't do, however, is challenge the other's pecking-order dominance. The masochistic warrior therefore prepares to battle by first con-ceding her subordinate position—analogous, ethologically, to

the animal who bares her throat—and only then denouncing
her conqueror, in effect saying, "Yes, you are the more dominant, stronger, and better fighter. But look at the damage you
have done to me."

The heart of the masochistic warrior's accusation is that
while the other may have power, he has been shameless in his
use of it. From the interpersonal standpoint of intimacy, few
allegations have such destructive impact on the other.

It is obvious that countertransference traps can be set by the
therapist as well as by the patient, and what I am about to relate
is an illustration of this. The time is about six months after
the publication of *Portrait of the Artist as a Young Patient* and
I am sitting in my office waiting eagerly for the arrival of Jessica, the first patient who has responded to a feature article
concerning my work with struggling artists that has just
appeared in a local newspaper. In my mind is a vision of a boun-
tiful crop of challenging, exciting, and different artists, which
will greatly enrich my existing practice. I think back to Jessica's
laughing introduction of herself to me on the telephone: "I
read the article on your book in the paper last Tuesday on artists
and narcissism. Well, my friends tell me the description fits
(laughs)." I recall that I thought her voice warm and mirthful,
and I am not embarrassed to admit to myself as I hear the door
bell ring that I hope she likes me.

The woman who greets me at the door is tall, proud-looking,
bohemianly dressed, attractive, and eating a pear. Upon entering the office, she smiles briefly, then turns casually away, in
search of a garbage can in which she can deposit the remains
of the pear. Only after taking care of that piece of business
does she seat herself on the couch for the first time, and begins by telling me that just prior to coming to see me, she had
picked up a couple of psychology books that were lying around
her apartment. One, R. D. Laing's *Knots*, which she almost

immediately put down: "I found it difficult, inaccessible." The other, which she liked, by Alfred Adler (she can't remember the title, but she quotes me a sentence or two), was "accessible." But the book by R. D. Laing, she seems to want to reemphasize, was "difficult."

It was at this early point in the session that I was prone to the suspicion that it might be she herself who is difficult, but I tried hard to block this out and listen to her story. It was a familiar young artist's story. She had come to New York City from out of town in order to be an actress and, in order to be available for auditions, immediately took a part-time job as a waitress. Three years later she was still a part-time waitress, a job she despised on her very first day of work and had continued to despise ever since. She is discouraged that acting jobs seemed so incredibly hard to come by, but she was even more discouraged that she was sharing a cramped apartment with two other women whom she did not particularly like, and that she did not seem to have a future. Most upsetting of all, however, were her relationships with men who, she felt, did not sufficiently respect her and—perhaps because they saw her as an inconsequential waitress—constantly tried to take advantage of her. As she saw it, her problem was that instead of standing up for herself she doubted herself, then blamed herself for what appeared to be wrong in the relationship, and only afterwards did she realize she should have trusted her instincts from the beginning.

Jessica paused at this point in her narrative, looking directly at me as though waiting for me to say something, and when I did not respond, she abruptly introduced the subject of her childhood (perhaps thinking that if she were to become more of a patient, I would become more of a therapist): alluding unhappily to a father who was emotionally never there for her, encounters as a teenager with physically abusive men, which she did not want to talk about, and her early interest in organizations founded to protect women from becoming the victims of violent men.

When she paused a second time, her look was considerably more direct and I could feel the weight of her demand that I intervene in some way on her behalf. While I sensed, on the one hand, that it was far too soon to offer what I would consider a cogent interpretation, I also understood that to maintain analytic neutrality would undoubtedly offend her. So I tried, somewhat uneasily, for a compromise. Referring to my work with struggling artists, which I knew was the original impetus for Jessica coming to see me, I reminded her of the similarities between what she had told me, and undoubtedly uniquely suffered, and the more universal plight of the young artist in our contemporary world. Although I recognized that what I said represented little more than therapeutic supportiveness, I was hoping that the link I was able to provide between her and all the actors and actresses I have treated would make her feel a little less alienated. But my half-hearted intervention spectacularly misfired. Examining me quizzically, Jessica, in a quiet, serious voice, asked, "Why did you say that?" In a halting voice, I replied that I intended to make her feel less isolated as an artist. She reflected on this briefly, and then— as though perhaps giving me a last chance to prove myself— sternly inquired, "Listen, if I were to come into therapy with you, what would you promise I could look forward to?"

No longer able to deny that we had gotten off to a dreadful start and that she was rapidly withdrawing, I was temporarily too disheartened to try to concoct on the spur of the moment a facile strategic answer to her unexpected challenge and I retreated instead into analytic silence.

Only a few, admittedly mutually anxious seconds passed, before Jessica rose to her feet. On her face was the determined look of a woman who has just arrived at an important decision. "Look," she said, as she opened her purse and withdrew some money, "how would it be if I left now and paid you twenty-five dollars for the session instead of fifty? I've only been here less than twenty minutes" (glancing at the clock on the bookcase shelf). "Would that be all right?"

In the demoralized state I was in, it seemed I was being asked to consent to my humiliation, so I replied, "No. This is a professional appointment. It is not let's-make-a-deal. We have an arrangement. Although I hope you stay for the entire session, you're free to leave whenever you want. But I am not reducing my rate."

Acting more determined than ever, Jessica strolled to the bookcase and pointedly placed the twenty-five dollars down on the shelf next to the clock. "Well, I'm leaving. Do you know how hard I have to work as a waitress in order to earn fifty dollars? And as far as I'm concerned even twenty-five dollars is wasted. As soon as I saw you I knew I was never coming back, so what's the point? My instincts are very good in these matters. And you know something? I feel very good about what I'm doing. I'm standing up for myself for a change!"

Feeling that I too must stand up for myself, I said, "I see you're very satisfied with yourself for ripping me off fifty percent of my fee. Remember, on the telephone, when you introduced yourself to me as a narcissist? You were right, and what you are doing now is an excellent example of your problem. You are feeling good about yourself, triumphant in fact, but it comes at the expense of causing another person—myself in this case, someone who only did his best to help you no matter how dissatisfied you were—to feel terrible. And that's the definition, Jessica, of a narcissistic triumph: to make yourself feel good by making someone else feel bad."

Well, it wasn't textbook technique, but then again I wasn't trying for that. All I was trying to do, all I was capable of doing in that particular painful situation, was to attempt to extricate myself from a countertransferential trap I had unconsciously fallen into: caring far too much for the approval of a patient who, it turned out, was narcissistically invested in destroying the perceived dominance of a male therapist.

In summary, the artificiality of the therapeutic situation, to a greater or lesser extent, engenders in the patient a certain unavoidable paranoia. Since so much of the everyday real is left out—no one person can possibly be that blessed with such saint-like acceptance of human foibles—patients cannot help but wonder what it would be like to experience the id and the superego of their therapist instead of just the working-alliance ego. They therefore set countertransference traps, and they do so for reasons not unlike those which compel them to engage in control games outside of therapy: they rely on the power of the particular strategy of control to evoke modeling behavior—that someone who acts confrontational, overly direct, needy, stubborn, complaining, and so on is likely to lure the other into a mirroring or defensive behavior. Although patients realize on some level that therapists who are drawn into a countertransference trap cannot be counted on because of their training—unless, of course, they lose their poise—to enact their need to counter-control, they nevertheless hope to instill in them an unambiguous desire to do so. In other words, patients are content to seduce the feelings of their therapists and in this regard are more than willing to accept one more non-reciprocal aspect of the therapeutic situation: they act out their conflicts, but their therapists act in.

There is a certain Machiavellian wisdom in this. As some-one who has had his share of getting caught in countertrans-ference traps (as does every therapist), I can say, in retrospect, that I acted in a way that I did not want to at the time. To be more precise, I certainly did not intend and did not want to feel the way I did about the track marks on my carpet, the dirt under my armchair, the patient who ridiculed my attractive-

ness to women, and the patient who proclaimed the worthless-
ness of my services, but I was simply unable to contain and
process my countertransference in a more therapeutic way. The
upshot and common aftermath, therefore, of perceiving that
you have just been indulging in such a countertransferential
enactment is to feel *diminished* as a therapist: all past self-doubts
and the therapist's negative identity, which secretly wonders if
you really have what it takes to help another person, are thereby
activated, which is, of course, the point of the transferential
enactment of a control game: to sabotage the true self of the
therapist and its symbolic, professional incarnation in the therapeutic situation.

It is worth noting that the control games we have alluded to
that patients transferentially enact, although clearly strategic,
are not thereby superficial. They are, more often than not, the
defensive product of a series of intrapsychic and interpersonal
losses. If the singles scene is a fertile soil for the study of control games that is because it is also a breeding ground for traumatic ruptures in intimacy. Not surprisingly, patients who come
into therapy to work on singles-scene issues report that they
have been interpersonally traumatized. What is interesting to
me, is that their traumas not only manifest a repetition compulsion, but also show a rather desperate attempt to transform
what perversely continues to feel shockingly new into something that feels old. And this, I believe, is because a key element
in the genesis of trauma is an antecedent denial: the prospect
of experiencing it, which seems unbearable, is foreclosed by
being protectively converted into the unthinkable. In other
words, the possibility of a certain traumatic experience happening to us is denied via the mechanism that somehow we
just cannot imagine its occurrence. And therein lies its malig-
nant power. Since we so effectively deny the possibility of
trauma before it strikes us as to be unable to conceive of it, we
do not need to further defend ourselves against it. When it does

unfortunately happen, we are therefore spectacularly unprepared to deal with it. Because we are so taken unaware we feel overwhelmed by an experience that in comparison to everything else we have known seems terrifyingly alien, and from that standpoint what the repetition compulsion aims to accomplish, in addition to a better-late-than-never mastery of uncontrollable anxiety, is to repeat a trauma in order to forget it.

Since the major traumatic events that befall most patients on the singles scene are rejection and abandonment, it is not surprising that the antecedent denial will focus there. Accordingly, patients who are unduly anxious over the possibility of breaking or losing a significant object relation are reassured that it cannot happen through the process of imagining just how devastating that would be to one or both parties. The sad truth, however—as those who are traumatically rejected or abandoned on the singles scene soon discover—is that most people, regardless of their dependency, have considerably more capability than is thought when it comes to breaking off a relationship. It may be, therefore, that a good part of the motivation for maintaining a highly ambivalent relationship is to not expose oneself to the dreadful experience of witnessing the potential for distancing that the other has: to live in a world in which you seemingly do not exist. And what is especially painful is to observe the immediate onset of survival strategies that spring into play as the now former relationship recedes from consciousness, as well as a sudden marshalling of new resources clearly meant to replace you. Perhaps most disheartening of all is the growing fear that—in contrast to George Bailey in *It's A Wonderful Life*—one will perceive that one's existential presence has made *no* difference because nothing seems to have changed in its absence.

Although the focus in the above examples, from the standpoint of the patients, was on "getting real" and "like it is," by no means were these the only control games that were enacted.

In fact, there are few patients who do not at one point or another transferentially play a number of the control games that have been depicted. And this is because it is almost impossible to be a patient and: to resist treatment without also being stubborn about it, to present symptoms without also complaining about them, to unconsciously activate specific defense mechanisms without also feeling defensive about what one is doing, and to be in therapy without role-playing that one is in therapy. There are endless and seamless opportunities for the patient to enact control games if he or she wants to and, in my view, the patient, at one time or another, *will* want to. The interested reader experienced in psychotherapy as either patient or therapist, who is willing to look for transferential manifestations of any or all of the control games that have been catalogued, should have no difficulty finding them.

In order to show to what extent the transferential enactment of control games can dominate the course of therapy, I will reintroduce Joel ("It's Fifty-Fifty") as a final clinical vignette.

JOEL (CONTINUED)

He was my *most* patient: the most afraid of women, of his mother, of his own anger, of tension, of losing control of his emotions, and, especially, of being controlled by hostile others. I first met him when I was doing intake interviews as part of a post-graduate program of advanced training in a therapy institute in New York City, and I remember being struck, as I shook hands with him, by his oddly arresting physical bearing. He was about six feet three inches tall, very gangly in build, bearded (he was teasingly referred to, at the time, as "Abe Lincoln" by a co-worker in the mailroom in which he worked), and with a long, melancholy face. He spoke in a very resonant although halting voice, and when he was anxious, he would begin to stutter slightly.

Otherwise, he sat obediently upright in his chair, quite still (he reminded me of a very young student sitting in a classroom) and, not initiating any conversation, patiently waited for me to ask each of the perfunctory questions I was obliged to ask in my capacity as an intake worker.

He was 37 years of age, single, had no attachments or friends, and had just been hired by a major motion picture company to work in their mailroom shortly after his unemployment insurance had run out. Two months prior to the intake appointment, in spite of his mother's shrieking protests and her dire prophecies of her son's imminent doom, Joel had moved out of the apartment they shared and for the first time in his life had rented a place of his own, a small studio in Queens. But so terrified had he been to defy the woman who seemed to exercise an iron hold on his psyche that he had managed to enlist his older brother, Teddy—who had moved out years ago and who considered Joel's departure to be long overdue—to literally stand guard by the door and guarantee him safe passage from his mother's anticipated fury as he walked out, bags in hand. As anxious as he was over living by himself, Joel did not consider that to be his presenting problem. What had driven him to seek out therapy was the growing sense of nervousness, sadness, and confusion as to what to do with his life, and fear of the future which he linked directly to the death of his father two years earlier.

On the intake form, there is a mandatory question in regard to the person's sexual history. Sensing just how uncomfortable the subject was likely to make him, I raised it as unthreateningly, matter-of-factly, and gingerly as I could. And Joel responded in a fairly straightforward fashion: he had had only one girlfriend in his life, someone who had actually picked him up in a delicatessen in mid-Manhattan, and that had occurred over fifteen years ago. He remembers being extremely tense about having sex with his girlfriend and how disappointed she appeared to be over his inability to achieve an erection, even though they had lain naked together on seven or eight separate occasions. Although every week he made a point of going to a singles bar—rarely staying for more than an hour, and usually for only five or ten minutes—he had not had a single date for at least five years. Guessing that he was perhaps skirting a simple but fundamental fact, and assuming, given my role as an intake worker, that we would probably never see each other again, I decided it was a safe risk to confront him very mildly. "Have you ever had sexual intercourse with a woman?" I asked. There was a long, memorable pause, during which I could simultaneously predict his answer and feel guilty for what I was about to put him through, and then, "N-n-n-o." (Subsequently, when I got to know him, and he began to trust me, Joel would confide in me more than once how my question had helped him to face the reality of his impotence: "I thought to myself, this is the guy who can help me.")

A week after the intake interview, I was surprised by the rather booming voice on the telephone reminding me of our recent encounter and informing me that the training institute for which I was conducting the intake interview had just assigned me to be his therapist. Right from the start, Joel struck me as an unusual and rather remarkable patient. I had never met anyone so sensitive, so terrified of the criticisms of others, so utterly convinced he was incapable of dealing with the slightest tension, and whose day-to-day existence seemed so filled with torment.

In fact, announcing that he had survived the day—"Well, I got through Wednesday. Two more days to go"—was often the way he would begin a session. I would ask him what it was he had to endure and Joel, in his way, would struggle between his need to be an obedient patient who did the right thing and his desperate desire to avoid talking about anything that made him feel in the least bit anxious. But I had no doubt that days for Joel were miseries and, accordingly, much of his therapy was devoted to damage control of the extreme psychic pain with which he habitually had to contend.

Slowly, over the course of time, perhaps bolstered by my obvious willingness to try to help him, Joel took me into his world, the world of an aimless, demoralized, 37-year-old mail-room employee who seemed incredibly tempting prey to any-one who wanted to bait him, and introduced me one by one to his oppressors. There first of all was Birdie, the loudmouthed, abusive woman who was in charge of the xerox room and who was fond of designating nicknames for new employees and who, in response to Joel's inquiry as to whether he had yet been nicknamed (thinking he was only joining in the fun), said, "Your name? You're El Stupido!"

It was Birdie whose unpredictable antics seemed to domi-nate much of Joel's waking consciousness, if only because she appeared to him to be socially fearless. She would say anything, do anything, and nobody could stand up to her and certainly not control her. There was, for example, the horrible time when she removed from a cabinet drawer a can of deodorant and began conspicuously spraying an area not ten feet from Joel, who had been working at a copying machine, after which she had glared in his direction and loudly proclaimed, "Someone, I'm not saying who, has just made a funky smell!" What astounded me about this incident, when I first heard it, far more than Birdie's sadistic boorishness, was Joel's uncanny ability to dissociate himself from an interpersonal situation, no matter how deeply and blatantly he was implicated in it, that he found unacceptable. Thus, in recounting it to me, after admitting he had been suffering from gas for much of the morning, had taken two trips to the bathroom for the express purpose of passing some gas, and had been alone with Birdie in the xerox room for at least half an hour prior to the inci-dent, he nevertheless managed to express seemingly genuine and profound puzzlement over whom Birdie was referring to in her remark. After discussing this with him, careful to indicate that it was an open question as to who or what had made the alleged funky smell, I raised the question of whether it was possible that Birdie, however mistakenly or insensitively, might have been referring to him. After a painful pause, in which he seemed to be wrestling with my point, Joel responded, shrugging his shoulders, "It's fifty-fifty."

This was his characteristic pattern whenever he imagined he had been slighted in public. He would under no circumstances ever address what had been said or done to him, retreating instead into a shell where he would speculate for hours on what might possibly have occurred, wracking his brains for scenarios that would get him off the hook. Thus, he would wonder if he might possibly have mistakenly heard what he thought he heard, if he had misinterpreted what he thought he had understood, if he had overreacted to something in reality that had been extremely minor, if he had taken something that was innocently and humorously meant in entirely the wrong way, and so on. Whenever Joel was certain he had heard something clearly and accurately, as he was, for example, in the incident of Birdie's remark about the perpetrator of a certain funky smell, he invariably believed that it was aimed at someone else. And whenever he thought or suspected that a suspicious remark or action was directed at him, he would as invariably be unable to recall whatever it was that had been said or done. Try as I might to help him reconstruct the interpersonal context, he would be unable—his fragile ego seemingly instantly repressing any unwelcome agents of tension or anxiety—to retrieve the telltale remark.

Thus, had Birdie been his sole nemesis, she would have been formidable enough. But there were others. There was Jenny, the assistant personnel manager, who sat in a glass-paneled office situated directly behind the spot where Joel customarily stood when he was working at the copying machine. Something about her aloof, precise manner and what Joel saw as phony politeness bugged him and, for a reason he did not understand, he felt uncomfortable standing with his back to her office. So he would periodically, as unobtrusively as he could, turn around and glance into her office to see if she really had been studying him as he suspected. And if by chance their eyes would meet, as they sometimes did, he would hesitate before looking away, to see if she were trying to stare him down. If she was staring at him, as he often thought she was, he would make his point the very next time he had to deliver a piece of mail to her office by silently approaching her in-basket, paying absolutely no attention to her, and taking his own sweet time about leaving. Once he may have taken too much time—walking slowly and deliberately to show that no one was going to make him hurry up—because suddenly behind his back, in a clear, audible whisper, he heard, "Get the hell out of my office" (but, of course, even though there was no one else in the office besides Jenny and himself, he did not think she was referring to him).

But he could never be sure whether people, for reasons he could not fathom, were secretly humiliating him. He was certain that in all the cases in which he wondered if someone might be mocking him, he, as he would always put it, "had done nothing wrong." He also knew that although most people were good, some were just mean. So when he had heard that someone who had worked for years in the mailroom was finally leaving, and had gone up to him, extending his hand in order to do the right thing, and saying, "I just want to say good-bye and wish you luck on your new job," he had heard laughter behind his back as he turned to go. Was that laughter directed at him? Had he perhaps been too nervous, too formal in what he had said? But he had done nothing wrong, so why should they laugh at him? He noticed that often he would deliver a piece of mail to an office or area in which several people had been previously talking and suddenly the conversation would stop, and, occasionally, as he walked away he would hear laughter or some sarcastic-sounding remark. Nor did it stop when he left the office—things would be said to him in the street, and dirty looks would be sent his way. Once a man in the street, who—although Joel himself did not think that he had been staring—obviously thought otherwise, had said in a very menacing voice, "Just keep your eyes straight ahead and don't stop moving if you know what's good for you." People in subway cars were forever inexcusably bumping into him, encroaching on his territory, sometimes violently pushing him out of their way. Even in the protected social getaway haven of Club Med he was not safe from abuse, for walking forlornly along the beach one evening, a burly man who was sitting with some friends on a blanket had commented out loud as he passed by, "That guy looks like he's light in the loafers." (With tears in his eyes, Joel explained to me that "light in the loafers means queer" and, as if to support his interpretation, he added that he once heard Johnny Carson jokingly refer to someone using the same expression.)

During the years that he was in therapy with me, there were at least three separate occasions when he was physically assaulted. Once, in the West Village, he was hit by a man—whom Joel at worst had slightly nudged as they crossed paths and then looked back to see if the man was staring at him—who had stopped, walked up behind Joel, and violently punched him in the shoulder, sending him lurching about ten feet down the block. Another time, when he happened to be mixing with the crowds who were attending a Shakespeare festival in Central Park, a teenage tough and what looked to be his younger brother ("who were looking for trouble," according to Joel) had passed him by. Perhaps ever so innocently, he had brushed shoulders with the younger boy, again glanced nervously backwards to see if anyone was looking at him, caught the two of them exchanging some words while looking in his direction, after which the older one shrugged his shoulders and started walking up to him. Panic-stricken and pretending not to have seen what he had just seen, Joel tried to meld with the surrounding crowd, but before he could, the bigger youth had reached his side and instantly thrown a vicious left hook to the body that sent him crashing to the ground. "Now why would he do that?" said a supportive elderly woman, who extended a hand to help Joel to his feet.

Although he was too afraid to go to a doctor, for several weeks after the incident with the teenage toughs Joel continued to rub the ribs on the left side of his body in therapy and to obsess aloud as to whether he might have sustained permanent damage. He was even more concerned the time he surprised me by arriving for his scheduled appointment with a discernible reddish splotch on the right side of his jaw, which seemed slightly swollen; he looked more downcast than I had perhaps ever seen him. "Do you know what just happened to me?" he asked rhetorically, and then proceeded to tell me. He had been walking in the vicinity of the Gulf and Western building, prior to taking a subway train in order to come to his therapy session. As this was the evening rush hour and crowds of people were milling about, he felt comparatively safe. In addition (this being the first of the three assaults), he had never before been physically attacked and the fact that this could actually happen to him was therefore unthinkable. So when the swarthy man, who looked to him like a South American arrogant young executive, and who for some unimaginable reason, seemed to be strangely staring at him from a distance of thirty feet away in the congested street, Joel did not see any apparent danger in briefly but pointedly staring back just to let him know that, in spite of the fact he was now a 39-year-old mailroom clerk, he had nothing to be ashamed about. And when the man, with a puzzled, annoyed look on his face, changing directions, began to walk up to him, Joel—who continued to look him evenly in the eye—was expecting anything except violence, anything except a quick punch to the jaw which knocked him to the pavement and left him asking fate and me why his had happened to him.

Why indeed? It was a therapeutic puzzle that Joel and I would ponder together for years. Part of the answer, I knew, lay in his bizarre relationship to his family. Other than the time he had solicited his brother's services as a bodyguard to help him move out of his mother's apartment, Joel had literally not spoken to Teddy for approximately ten years. In fact, a code of silence and a mutual understanding had grown up between them that each was expected to treat the other as a social leper. At no time and under no circumstances were they ever to acknowledge each other's presence, to engage in conversation, and, especially, to meet face-to-face in the home of their mother. Thus, if Teddy were to visit on a Saturday afternoon, word would be passed through the mother, Irene, of the time of the visit, the time when Joel was expected not to be present. And should there be a mishap, as there sometimes was, and Joel, for whatever reason, would return earlier than expected from an afternoon movie, greet his mother and then, to his horror, hear the sound of his brother in the kitchen, he might—after a deadly silence—also hear the fury of Teddy's fist pounding the table as he cried out, "*Why, Why* is he here!" (Amazingly, at least to me, whenever I would invite Joel to speculate on the traumatic events that must have led up to such displays of psychotic-like rage on the part of his brother, Joel, invariably shrugging, would reply, "I have no idea.")

The linchpin of his family dynamics, however, was his symbiotic relationship to his mother, undoubtedly, from the standpoint of his fragile psyche, the most important, forceful, and terrifying person in his universe. Not once in the seven years

I had known him had he ever reported raising his voice to his mother above the mild-mannered, childlike, obedient tone he evidently felt was demanded of him in his self-appointed, life-long role of being "the good son." Not that he was oblivious to the almost constant frustration he experienced whenever he had dealings with his mother, especially when he incited her stubbornness and willfulness by disagreeing with her in any way. And not that he was unable to freely ventilate his hostility towards her within the safety of therapy and the despair he, increasingly, retrospectively felt whenever he revisited how she treated him as a child: regarding him almost as a creature without feelings or wishes of his own that were of consequence whose function was to do whatever he was told to do without questioning it (e. g., "pick up my bra over there for me, Joel, will you?"); who once bragged to a next-door neighbor, "I always wanted a daughter and I got one," and who would boisterously wave away any attempts on Joel's part to express some of the torture that was his daily life with the demeaning reassurance, "You? There's nothing wrong with you!" Not surprisingly, the one thing he would never do—even when his mother in the last years of her life was confined to a wheelchair, disabled by Alzheimer's disease and evidencing the mind of "a 5-year-old"— was to assert that he was a person of worth, that he had a self to be reckoned with, that he was taking responsibility for a life not meant to be lived for her insatiable gratification.

Regarding the reign of terror that Joel appeared to live under from a host of oppressors, I had no doubt that it was not delusional. While he had pronounced paranoid trends, occasional ideas of reference, a fantastic ability to dissociate himself from and to distort unwanted, tension-filled interpersonal situations, I was quite sure that office co-workers *did* laugh at him behind his back, that Jenny *had* stage-whispered, "Get the hell out of my office," and that impulsive, aggressive men and delinquent teenagers, infuriated by his puzzling, detached staring, might knock him to the ground. The key, however, to understanding the peculiar dynamics of his driven inner life, I realized, would come from unravelling the transference–countertransference transactions between us.

In the course of therapy, Joel gradually became aware and often told me that I was the second most important person in the world to him after his mother, and the one person he could trust above all others. There were numerous signs that this was true. He regularly confided to me things that he would not dream of telling to anyone else. Compared with the states of sometimes phenomenal tension that he often complained about, his demeanor in therapy seemed vastly more relaxed. He never came close to achieving peace of mind, of course, but he often would clown around, crack old vaudeville jokes, kibitz a little, lapsing on occasions when he perceived himself to be talking in a particularly nervous, herky-jerky way, into an instant (near professional) impression of his favorite comedian, Jackie Mason, "So, I say this, I say that, I mean do this!" When he was in what he himself considered a good mood, I could hear him humming or singing softly on the landing outside my office door. Once in a while, he would arrive at an insight by himself, make a surprising connection between disparate events, thoughts, or feelings, or ponder deeply the meaning of his unquestionably forlorn existence. And there were times, after what we both agreed was an inspiring session, when he would trudge out of the office looking for all the world, and at least momentarily convincing me that he was a soldier of therapy, ready to do battle with the demons of his mind.

But over the years I was increasingly forced to admit that such flashes of improvement, working-alliance comraderie and flights into health were at best short-lived if not illusory. Far more significant were his repressed anger or rage, his incredible stubbornness (not unlike his mother's), his perverse refusal to respect and ally himself in any manner with his life instincts.

And, of course, because not once in seven years did he ever raise his voice in anger to me, strongly disagree with me, or not speak to me with exaggerated deference—in spite of his genuine and considerable affection for me—I realized that much of his rage and hatred for life was directed at me.

Since Joel was perhaps more terrified of his negative transference than any patient I had ever worked with, he could never dare to be directly critical of me in even the mildest of ways. But as soon as he had seated himself on the couch, he would persistently kick at pieces of lint or any minute object lying on the carpet in the place where his feet would normally rest, which in his judgment (as he explained to me years later) "didn't belong there." Although he was the most punctual patient I had ever known, rarely deviating by more than 30 seconds from the exact time of his scheduled appointment, he made a point of lingering for several minutes at the end of each session, usually by going to the bathroom (he also held the record among my patients for using my bathroom the most) sometimes simply to comb his hair, groom himself, and look at himself in the mirror (often doing this with the door wide open) prior to going out in public. He was in addition perhaps the most silent patient I had experienced, but there was nothing therapeutic in the use he made of the silence that was provided: he did not muse, he did not introspect, he did not attempt to make contact with his self in some deeper way. Instead, as he put it, he would "take a break" from talking, reward himself for the few words he had said, and vanish into a kind of limbo of vegetative withdrawal.

Or he would sit immovable and dazed-looking on the couch, sometimes with a flicker of a grandiose smile on his face. At such times, when he seemed hopelessly distant from me, his fingers might slowly become steepled together, in a gesture of schizoid condescension. So dissociated was his manner of relating at these times that it took me years to realize that often—

when I believed that Joel was moodily and meaninglessly staring in space—he was in fact staring at me, unconsciously converting the holding environment into a paranoid basic training site wherein he could symbolically duel with a variety of imagined persecutory others. And once, when I had become too uncomfortably aware of his intense staring to ignore it, yet unable to think of a therapeutic way to broach so delicate an issue, I simply said, "We seem to be staring at one another," Joel then utterly surprised me by being about as relieved as I had ever seen him. "Yeah," he sighed and proceeded to reveal to me how for years he had suspected that I had been staring at him, trying to stare him down, and he had often fantasized about what it would be like to stare me down.

My gradual awareness of my own discomfort with Joel's staring put me in touch with other countertransferential irritations. I had never liked his habit of kicking and scraping his shoes on my carpet as soon as he had settled himself on the couch. At times, the refusal of me that underlay his silence became almost palpable and I could not help but take it personally. Once when he was recounting how he had declined to answer a fellow employee's question as to whether he celebrated a particular Jewish holiday—justifying it to me with one of his favorite expressions, "It's none of his business"—and remembering how incredibly withholding he could be when it came to communicating psychic news about himself, I suddenly and unhappily realized, "My God, he's been telling me to mind my own business for the last four years!"

By far my greatest countertransferential difficulty, however, concerned dealing with my own limitations when it came to helping Joel with his. I don't think I ever worked as hard to help anyone, and in such good faith, as I did with Joel, yet never was I so spectacularly ineffectual on so many levels. It was not just that in the seven years he was in therapy with me, he had only a handful of token dates, never had a girlfriend, never made love, never had successful intercourse, found a friend, really enjoyed himself, made a plan, or manifested the slightest desire to enhance his self-proclaimed wretched existence. He never in any meaningful way *tried to fight for himself*. He lived literally on a moment-by-moment basis and the principle by which he conducted his life was that all tension was bad and all reduction of tension was good. And I did not seem to be able to get him to see beyond that.

What did help, however, was *for me* to better understand the source of my frustration. I had prided myself on my therapeutic personality, on being adept when it came to quickly reassuring a mistrustful patient and providing the rudiments of a potential holding environment. Like every psychoanalytic psychotherapist, I hoped to be able to facilitate the growth of new self-enhancing psychic structures, but I did not mind being, for long periods of time if that is all I could be, an auxiliary ego or a supportive presence to a patient who required it. What I did very much mind was someone *insisting*, as Joel did, that I become an auxiliary ego.

For I gradually came to understand that on a primitive level Joel was engaged in a kind of symbolic mental combat with a world that was perceived as a malign mother who was shirking her duty, which was to symbiotically live his life for him. And Joel was determined that if he could not find someone or some force to live his life for him, he would absolutely refuse to do it by himself. It was this refusal, I believed, far more than any other single psychic impairment, that kept him so developmentally frozen. With fantastic willfulness he was continuing to treat himself, as his mother had, as a person almost devoid of an autonomous psyche. (Christopher Bollas's [1987] ideas concerning the "self as object" were especially useful to me here.)

Seeing that, I could also see how I had been countertransferentially colluding. In my insistence that he address and take some existential responsibility for the core issues of his life, I was, in effect, regardless of how therapeutic my ultimate intentions may have been, trying to live his life for him by instilling a passion for living that could only come from him, or not at all. In my own way, I was being as stubborn as he was and, moreover, by so doing, I was treating him as though he utterly lacked autonomy, as though the only way he could become autonomous was if I made him so.

I therefore began to treat Joel in a new way, as an entirely separate and, his massive psychic impoverishment notwithstanding, autonomous being. I pretty much told him what I have just written here: that I could not function as a magical symbiotic mother who would direct how his life would be lived, even if I wanted to; that I believed that he was considerably more capable of dealing with tension than he apparently did, but that he was determined to treat himself more or less as his mother had treated him. And I saw no reason not to tell him just how incredibly, self-destructively stubborn I thought he was. All of which, through countless repetitions over time, became condensed into three simple interpretations which Joel readily took: (1) "This is your stubbornness," (2) "As you know, I think you're tougher and could take a lot more tension than you do," and (3) "Now you're treating yourself like your mother did—as a helpless child."

I used to think that Joel was well on his way to becoming the kind of patient whom Kernberg (1986) once referred to as a "lifer": someone healthy enough to recognize that there was a real need for therapy, but too sick to sufficiently benefit from it so as to be able to terminate. But one day, after seven years of intensive psychotherapy, Joel walked into my office and announced that out of the blue, the major motion picture company for which he still worked had just announced that it was uprooting in a month and relocating to Los Angeles, and taking along all current employees who were similarly inclined.

With an excited grin, Joel announced that he had decided to accept the invitation to relocate with his company and that, thanks to therapy, he felt ready for what promised to be "the adventure of my life."

That was how Joel's therapy, after seven years, ended. But before it did, I had managed to let go of my need to intervene in his fate: if his frustration at not being able to control a ubiquitous, malign mother was so great that he was willing to spite his self by becoming the greatest existential non-achiever he was capable of, so be it! There was nothing I could do and this truth, as they say, set both of us free. For there were many moments in the year and a half or so before his departure when I was able to observe a considerably more relaxed and expressive Joel. Although he still did not have a clue as to which direction he wanted his life to go, there was no doubt that when he was at least temporarily released from this torment, he could be oddly humorous, gentlemanly, articulate, sensitive, creatively offbeat, and warmly personal. Now I could see at least the outline of a definite style of being and although I had no idea as to how, if at all, he would elaborate it, I could say at last that I had broken through, made contact with, and achieved a real glimpse of his emergent true self.

Finally, it is one more countertransference trap to believe, as therapists, that we can deal with our fear of not meeting our patients' incessant demands that we take charge of their destiny by arming ourselves with more and better techniques. It is perhaps wiser instead and more liberating to recognize the pervasiveness of a patient's transferential enactments of control games and the countertransference traps that they set for their therapists. To let go of the desires not to be controlled by patients, to control their desire to control us, and to too benignly control the progress of therapy can only lead to a greater availability for the real work that lies ahead.

REFERENCES

Alper, G. (1992). *Portrait of the Artist as a Young Patient.* New York: Insight/Plenum.
—— (1993). The theory of games and psychoanalysis. *Journal of Contemporary Psychotherapy* 23(1):47–60.
—— (1994a). *The Singles Scene.* San Francisco-London: International Scholars Publications.
—— (1994b). *The Puppeteers.* New York: Fromm International Publishing Corporation.
Bateson, G., Jackson, D. D., Haley, J., and Weakland, J. H. (1955). Towards a theory of schizophrenia. *Behavioral Science* 4:251–264.
Berne, E. (1964). *Games People Play.* New York: Grove.
Bion, W. R. (1970). *Attention and Interpretation.* London: Tavistock.
—— (1981). *Emotional Turbulence. Clinical Seminars and Four Papers,* pp. 223–233. Reading, England: Radavian Press.
—— (1992). *Cogitations.* London and New York: Karnac.
Bollas, C. (1987). *The Shadow of the Object.* New York: Columbia University Press.
—— (1992). *Being a Character.* New York: Hill and Wang.
—— (1995). *Cracking Up.* New York: Hill and Wang.
Dawkins, R. (1986). *The Blind Watchmaker.* New York: Norton.
—— (1995). *River Out of Eden.* New York: Basic Books.
Farber, L. (1976). *Lying, Despair, Jealousy, Envy, Sex, Suicide, Drugs And The Good Life.* New York: Basic Books.
Fenichel, O. (1941). *Problems of Psychoanalytic Technique.* New York: Psychoanalytic Quarterly.
Freud, S. (1900). The interpretation of dreams. *Standard Edition* 4 & 5.
Gleick, J. (1987). *Chaos.* New York: Viking Penguin.
—— (1992). *Genius.* New York: Random House.
Haley, J. (1958). An interactional explanation of hypnosis. In *Therapy, Communication And Change,* vol. 1, Human Com-

munication Series, ed. D. D. Jackson. Palo Alto, CA: Science and Behavior Books, 1968.

Horney, K. (1950). *Neurosis And Human Growth*. New York: Norton.

Jackson, D. D. and Haley, J. (1963). Tranference revisited. In *Therapy, Communication and Change*, vol. 1, Human Communication Series, ed. D. D. Jackson, pp. 115–129. Palo Alto, CA: Science and Behavior Books, 1968.

Kernberg, O. (1975). *Borderline Conditions And Pathological Narcissism*. New York: Jason Aronson.

—— (1986). Technical strategies in the treatment of narcissistic personalities. In *Severe Personality Disorders*, pp. 197–209. New Haven, CT: Yale University Press.

Kohut, H. (1971). *The Analysis of the Self*. New York: International Universities Press.

Laing, R. D. (1970). *Knots*. New York: Pantheon.

Lorenz, K. (1982). *The Foundation of Ethology*. New York: Simon and Schuster.

—— (1991). *Here Am I—Where Are You? The Behavior of the Greylag Goose*. Florida: Harcourt Brace Jovanovich.

Phillips, A. (1993). *On Kissing, Tickling and Being Bored*. Cambridge, MA: Harvard University Press.

—— (1994). *On Flirtation*. Cambridge, MA: Harvard University Press.

Sartre, J.-P. (1956). *Being and Nothingness*. New York: Simon and Schuster.

Shapiro, D. (1965). *Neurotic Styles*. New York: Basic Books.

Spitz, R. A. (1965). *The First Year of Life*. New York: International Universities Press.

Sullivan, H. S. (1953). *The Interpersonal Theory of Psychiatry*. New York: Norton.

—— (1973). *Clinical Studies in Psychiatry*. New York: Norton.

Winnicott, D. W. (1960). Ego distortion in terms of true and false self. In *The Maturational Processes and the Facilitating Environment*. New York: International Universities Press.

—— (1969). Use of an object and relating through identification. In *Playing and Reality*. New York: Basic Books, 1971.

Wittgenstein, L. (1953). *Philosophical Investigations*. New York: MacMillan.

INDEX